Recording Tips for Music Educators

Essential Music Technology: The Prestissimo Series
Richard McCready, *Series Editor*

Digital Organization Tips for Music Teachers
Robby Burns

Recording Tips for Music Educators
A Practical Guide for Recording School Groups
Ronald E. Kearns

Recording Tips for Music Educators

A Practical Guide for Recording School Groups

Ronald E. Kearns

OXFORD
UNIVERSITY PRESS

Oxford University Press is a department of the University of Oxford. It furthers the University's objective of excellence in research, scholarship, and education by publishing worldwide. Oxford is a registered trade mark of Oxford University Press in the UK and certain other countries.

Published in the United States of America by Oxford University Press
198 Madison Avenue, New York, NY 10016, United States of America.

Library of Congress Cataloging-in-Publication Data
Names: Kearns, Ronald E., 1952– author.
Title: Recording tips for music educators : a practical guide for recording
school groups / by Ronald E. Kearns.
Description: New York, NY, United States of America : Oxford University
Press, [2017] | Series: Essential music technology : the prestissimo
series | Includes bibliographical references and index.
Identifiers: LCCN 2016043762| ISBN 9780190465230 (pbk : alk paper) |
ISBN 9780190465254 (epub)
Subjects: LCSH: Sound—Recording and reproducing. | Music—Instruction and
study—Audio-visual aids.
Classification: LCC TK7881.4 .K3955 2017 | DDC 781.49071—dc23
LC record available at https://lccn.loc.gov/2016043762

9 8 7 6 5 4 3 2 1

Printed by Webcom, Inc., Canada

To Lillie and Tiffany

Contents

Foreword

Recording is an art—as much of an art as teaching itself. It requires knowledge, musicianship, problem-solving strategies, listening skills, and patience, just like teaching.

Many teachers feel overwhelmed with the idea of recording their groups, as music education classes at undergraduate or graduate level have often included nothing more than a cursory glance at recording skills, if at all. Teachers know that being able to capture a good recording of their groups will have immediate benefits for their ensembles—parents, students, teachers, coaches, and private instructors can listen to recordings and aid the process of refining and developing musical skills.

However, how do teachers know the best ways to capture the performance? How do they know what microphones to choose? How do they know where to place the microphones? How do they know how to edit and master the recording? How do they prevent the noise of the lights and the air conditioning spoiling the recording? How do they record successfully in unfriendly acoustic spaces such as the gymnasium or the outdoor auditorium? These questions often loom large in the director's preparation and hamper the work needed to get ready for concerts or rehearsals, and they usually manifest as just one more thing on the endless to-do list of the typical music teacher.

Without a good knowledge of recording skills, teachers often find themselves having to make do with a poor recording of their ensembles, or no recording at all, or even having to pay someone else to make the recording for them. When you listen back to the recording and find it is poor quality, you realize you cannot make the students go back and repeat their performance. In the world of live school music, one take is all you get, and if it's a bad take, it's too late to do anything about it.

The *Prestissimo* series of books aims to take the fear out of technology applications in the music classroom. Each volume deals with a separate area of music technology, and is written by a proven expert in the field who is also a successful and respected music teacher. All the books provide handy, easily digestible tips to enable music teachers to feel comfortable with technology and use it to their advantage as they continue to focus on their main goal of making excellent musical experiences for students.

Ron Kearns, the author of "Recording Tips for Music Educators" is a highly respected band teacher, adjudicator, and clinician. He has had a long and successful career training and coaching bands and orchestras of the highest quality. Much of his success comes from the use of recording in his classroom, and his ability to capture excellent recordings of his ensembles is aided by over thirty years experience in working in professional studios. Ron is equally passionate about recording as he is about directing and teaching, and has spent his entire career as music teacher/band director by day, producer/audio engineer by night and on weekends. His experience in both worlds sets him apart as an extraordinary musician. Ron's bands sound good because they can learn from a master educator who is able to record his ensembles well and use those recordings to inform and enhance learning.

Our hope is that in these pages, you will be able to find exactly the information you need to become a good recording engineer in your classroom and auditorium, without being overwhelmed by the complexities of the recording art. This book will likely become a vade mecum for all teachers who wish to employ recording as a vital tool in their instructional strategies toolshed. Your students will benefit from hearing good recordings, your ensembles will improve with being able to hear and evaluate themselves, and for you, engineering an excellent recording will no longer seem an impossible to-do on the never-ending concert-day preparation list.

Richard McCready
Series Editor

Acknowledgments

Writing a book is a solitary task that could not be achieved without a lot of help from others. I'd first like to thank Lillie B. Kearns, Tiffany A. Kearns, and Ida K. Adams for reading and proofing my first few drafts and encouraging me throughout the process. I'd like to thank Richard McCready for coming to me to ask me to write a book for music educators from a music educator's view, using my experience with recording as background. Over the years I've had a chance to work with and get to know some very good recording engineers. They were willing to share their wisdom and experience with me for this book. Thanks to Dr. Benjamin Tomassetti, Bob Dawson, and Jon T. Miller for answering my questions on live or remote recording. Jon and I have recorded choirs, bands, and orchestras live and he was the first engineer to record my orchestras and bands. Thanks to Mike Monseur of Bias Recording and Mastering Studios, and Charlie Pilzer and Mike Petillo of Airshow Mastering Studios, for sharing pictures of their mastering studios. Thanks to Gloria Dawson for allowing me to use photographs of Bias Recording Studios. Thanks to Davida Rochman of Shure Incorporated, Matthias Spahrmann of Neumann Berlin, Micah Eberman of ZOOM, Phil Tennison of Marshall Electronics and Mogami Cables, Larry Seiler of Los Senderos Studio, and Cliff Castle of Audix Corporation for providing me with illustrations and photos to share. Lastly, I'd like to thank Norman Hirschy for his willingness to answer my questions and offer guidance along the way. Thanks to God for giving me strength to complete this project.

As I said in my first book, if you see a turtle on a fencepost you know he didn't get up there by himself. This book could not have been completed without the help of these special people and others not named. Thank you all for lifting me up to that fencepost!

Introduction

When I was discussing what I wanted this book to be with my editor, I was very happy to discover that he and I were in agreement. This book is not a book for the weekend recording enthusiast or recording hobbyists. The purpose of this book is to give help and guidance to music educators who want to record their groups for educational purposes and to preserve an audio history of their groups' performances. There are plenty of blogs, websites, and books available for the hobbyists to access.

Music educators are generally not trained to record their groups, even though it's an important aspect of what they do. Giving students an opportunity to objectively listen to and critique their performances is an important part of the learning process. Once students have an opportunity to evaluate themselves, they gain an understanding of what the director has been trying to achieve during rehearsals. Recording rehearsals is an important part of the process. Students can track their progress and compare each step from the initial preparation to the final performance.

During my thirty years as a music educator I had many guided listening exercises with my students as we evaluated our performances. Some of our performances were recorded with tape recorders set up in an auditorium or in the rehearsal room. Most of the recordings only recorded the most dominant sounds, so we never got an accurate view of what we sounded like. Fortunately, my school districts hired professional recording engineers to come in and record our festivals and assessments. My students and I were able to hear the most intricate parts clearly.

While working as an educator, I was also working as an independent record producer. I became very much aware of microphone styles, types, and polar patterns. I also became aware of cables, stands, and setups. I had an engineer who was a parent come in and record my group. It was then that I realized I could combine my passions. I went to the Peabody Institute, now part of Johns Hopkins University, to study studio and remote recording during summer sessions. Combined with what I'd learned from observing engineers in the studio, I got what I needed to effectively record my group. My school went through a renovation and auditorium construction, so I was able to order a sound-board and multiple microphones. Because of my experience I was able to get quality recordings of my group.

I am sharing what I've learned through trial and error, from talking to and observing engineers, and what I learned in recording classes with you in this book. There are very few things as valuable as a good recording of your group. Good luck!

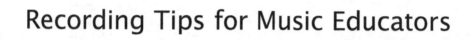

Recording Tips for Music Educators

Getting Started Recording Your Group

What are my first steps?

It would seem obvious that the first steps for recording your group should be planning and organizing, but in case it isn't, let's address planning as your first step here. The reason some recordings are poorly done has nothing to do with equipment; it's poor planning and poor microphone placement. Planning means sitting down and listing or outlining what you want to achieve and working out a step-by-step way of achieving your goal. You can't step in an hour before a rehearsal or performance, put microphones up, and then hit "record." You have to know about the nature of your group, the acoustics of the room, proximity of microphones, and how not to record incidental or ambient sounds. To prepare well, you should take notes during normal rehearsals. You'll be able to use your notes and observations to give you a good outline for what you hope to avoid and what you hope to achieve. For instance, if your brass section is much stronger than your woodwinds, you'll need to compensate for that. If you have more sopranos than basses or altos, you may need to adjust their positions or microphone positions to compensate for that. If the room has tile floors or cinderblock walls, you'll need to compensate for that (otherwise brass and percussion will dominate the recording). Microphone placement can compensate for most of these problems if you plan ahead. The old adage "we'll fix it in the mix" does not apply here. For most live band, orchestra, or chorus performances, you will not be recording on multiple tracks. Simply stated, what goes in comes out.

Because different microphones do different things, you need to know a little about the different kinds of microphones and microphone polarities. There are three basic microphone polar patterns: cardioid, supercardioid, and hypercardioid. These patterns are used in unidirectional microphones. All three of these patterns exclude off-axis and

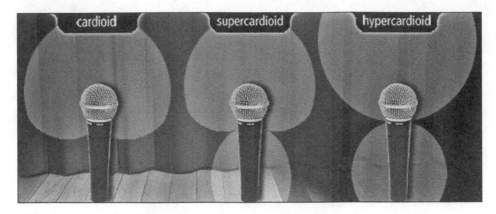

FIGURE 1.1 Microphone polar patterns. Copyright Shure Incorporated; used with permission.

rear-axis sounds coming from behind the microphone or from the sides (null points). Null points are the parts of a polar pattern that don't record sounds. The polar pattern is the shape of a microphone's field of sensitivity. This means the directions from which it ignores or accepts incoming sounds. Omnidirectional microphones respond to sounds coming from all directions. Bidirectional microphones pick up sounds from east and west while excluding sounds from north and south. A unidirectional microphone primarily collects sounds from one direction and excludes sounds from other directions. Figure 1.1 illustrates polar patterns.

Choosing the right microphones will help the recording process go smoothly. There are microphones that can be used to pick up all sounds in a general location, and there are microphones you can use to target specific sections of the group you're recording. School budgets often dictate what kinds of microphones and the number of microphones you can get.

Recording engineers rely on their experience to choose the right microphones; if you can consult one before purchasing microphones, do it. If not, familiarize yourself with the information provided here. You don't need to purchase a high-end studio microphone to get a good recording. Those microphones require additional equipment, like preamps, in order to power the microphone to take full advantage of the quality of the microphone. Each piece of equipment represents money from your overall budget. Ribbon microphones (the lowest choice for recording large groups) are microphones that don't work well with snare drums or a heavy hitting drummer because the ribbon can literally break.

Microphone placement

After you've done your homework and made preparations, you're ready to set up for the recording. Later in the book I'll discuss microphone brands and how to select the ones that are best for your recording environment, but for now I'll simply discuss placement.

I was fortunate that before I studied recording techniques, one of my band parents was a professional recording engineer. After a concert he approached me about recording my groups. When he came in and started setting up microphones, I discovered how little I knew about recording. One of the things you should do is poll your school community to see if there are any audio professionals there. If so, let them assist you; if not, follow the suggestions that are in this book. Figure 1.2 shows good microphone placement. Figure 1.3 shows poor or bad placement.

Besides the performance, microphone placement is the most important thing that will determine the quality of your live recording. Depending on the size of the group, microphone placement and microphone proximity will vary. For large groups, certain microphone placements can be used to capture the whole sound source (concert band, orchestra, guitar ensemble, jazz ensemble, or large chorus). Trying different distances from the group after doing a few test tracks will help. Sometimes you may want to take advantage of the acoustics to get a natural mix and balance of your group. Sometimes

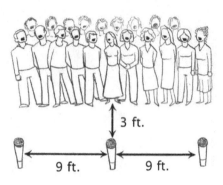

Good Distance Ratio

FIGURE 1.2 Microphone set-up spacing for choral groups good distance ratio. Copyright Shure Incorporated; used with permission.

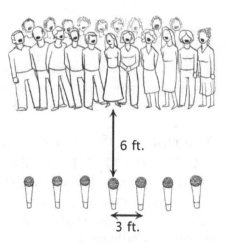

Bad Distance Ratio

FIGURE 1.3 Microphone set-up spacing for choral groups bad distance ratio. Copyright Shure Incorporated; used with permission.

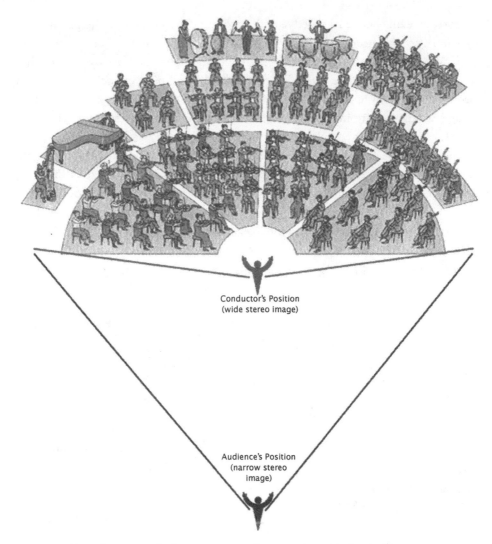

Conductor's Position
(wide stereo image)

Audience's Position
(narrow stereo image)

FIGURE 1.4 Microphone setup for large instrumental groups. Copyright Scoringfilms.net.

you may want to direct the microphones toward a section or group of instruments that may not carry as well as others because of timbre or weak players. Engineers call this finding the sweet spot. Figure 1.4 depicts a setup for a large instrumental group.

Description of microphone recording techniques and microphone placement

After considering the things previously mentioned, you're now ready to choose the best technique for setting up and recording your group. Size of the group and recording space will figure in. Before choosing which technique to use, you first must identify and describe those techniques. They are a parallel pair of microphones (a matched pair, same type, same polar pattern) pointing directly ahead; X/Y technique or mid-side technique;

ORTF, also known as side-other-side technique (Office de Radiodiffusion Télévision Française); and Decca tree technique. The most preferred is the X/Y technique, which uses two cardioid microphones placed at 90 degree angles. The result of this setup is that the microphone on the right picks up the left side of the room and the microphone on the left picks up the right side of the room. There is a refinement of this technique called the Blumlein pair (mid-side) which uses a mid-microphone and a bidirectional microphone. The result of using this technique is that one microphone will pick up the sound source directly, and the bidirectional microphone picks up sounds from the side. Figure 1.5 shows a mid-side recording setup.

The set-up distance is exactly the same as the X/Y, except for the fact that you are using a bidirectional microphone. The Blumlein pair is known for creating an exceptionally realistic stereo image, but that image is dependent on the size of the sound source as well as the quality of the room. If ORTF is used, microphones should be matched or very similar and should be placed seventeen centimeters apart at a 110-degree angle. The Decca tree setup uses five microphones, three setup in a T pattern and an "outrigger" pair set up further to the right and left. The T faces the band or orchestra with a center microphone, one microphone facing right and one microphone facing left. The outrigger pair should be spaced no wider than the width of the group. Figure 1.6 shows this setup.

For large groups, a stereo pair of microphones five (5) feet above and six (6) feet back should capture the whole source. When using a stereo pair, it's important that the

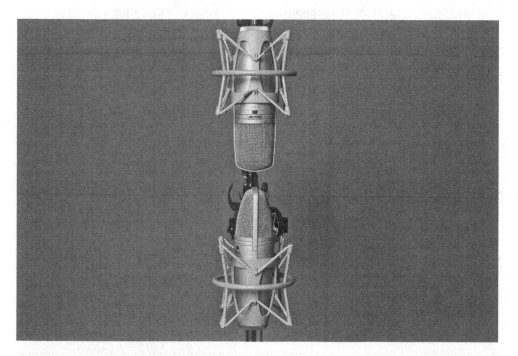

FIGURE 1.5 Mid-side recording setup with a matching pair of Shure microphones. Copyright Shure Incorporated; used with permission.

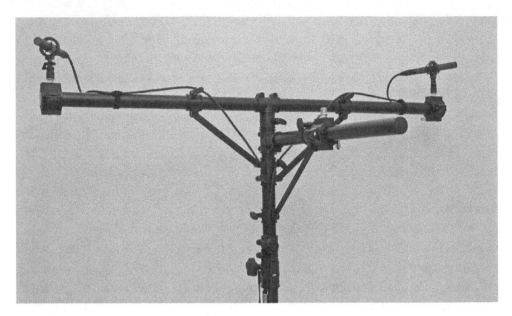

FIGURE 1.6 Decca tree microphone setup with stand. Photo by Jim Miller.

two microphones match (i.e., that they are the same model). You can use a fifteen-foot microphone stand if you'd like to avoid unwanted sound sources (programs rattling, coughs, etc.). This recording technique is based on the ORTF technique. The idea is to capture the sound as if the microphones are your ears. Figure 1.7 shows stereo pairs.

Many acoustic instruments radiate up and out into the room, so you can capture them with a good mix of air. For live performances this is called ambience, and the live recording gives the listener the sensation of being in the room. The recording "breathes" and does not lose the live quality and sound stagnant.

When recording in the rehearsal room, my preferred microphone placement position is just behind and over the conductor's podium. In an auditorium I prefer using a fifteen-foot microphone stand with a stereo pair bracket on the floor off the stage or microphones hanging from the ceiling. Once again, advanced planning helps you to decide what's best for your group. This is not a one-size-fits-all situation; you must experiment and let your ears decide. You may want to have your group expand or become a little compact. You may want to put the microphones on stage behind the podium. Your ears will tell you what's best for your group.

With smaller groups, you may want to place the microphones closer to the sound source. If your group is a well-balanced group, acoustical ambience can be achieved using the large ensemble setup (Decca tree). If not, you may want to use a directional microphone that you can point at sections and omnidirectional microphones that can pick up the sound in the room. For this you'll be recording multiple tracks and after the recording, you'll have to mix in postproduction to get the desired sound. This may sound intimidating, but it's exactly what you do as a conductor during a live performance.

The difference is that you're doing it on a mixing board that you can control: If you need more clarinet, you can bring up the clarinet level; if you need less trumpet, drop it down in the mix. The reason microphone placement is important is that microphones are collecting the sounds you'll be working with later. With two-track stereo recording you record exactly what you mix as the conductor during the performance. With multiple microphones you're recording tracks you're going to manipulate electronically later. Once again, this is no different from what you're trying to achieve from the podium.

As I mentioned earlier, one of the best ways to get a very good stereo recording is to use a refinement on the X/Y technique and ORTF, called mid-side recording. The mid-side pattern covers a wider field. Mid-side is a coincident technique, which means both microphones are put as closely together as possible. It uses a mid-microphone that is aimed at the sound source and a bidirectional microphone to pick up sound from the

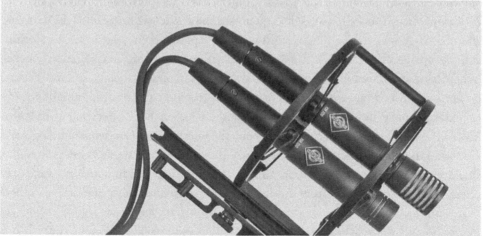

FIGURE 1.7 Matching pair of parallel microphones 6.7-inch distance. Used with permission of Neumann. Berlin.

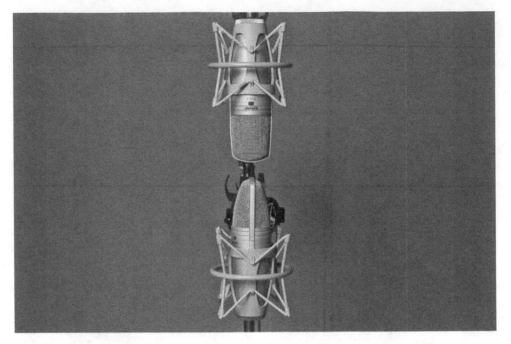

FIGURE 1.8 Mid-side recording setup. Copyright Shure Incorporated; used with permission.

sides. This type of recording requires the use of a mixer to decode the signals. I'll discuss it in more detail later as it applies to recording in rooms of different sizes. Figure 1.8 shows a matching pair of microphones set in a mid-side (M/S) pattern.

Most school budgets will support the purchase and use of dynamic microphones. Dynamic microphones are very versatile and are ideal for school recordings. They use a coil of wire and a magnet to create an audio signal. These microphones are less expensive and more rugged. Since students will possibly be handling these microphones, durability is important. They're not as high in quality as the condenser microphones I'll discuss later, but they will yield a good recording. I'm purposely trying not to get too technical, but a brief explanation is needed to help you understand the difference between dynamic microphones and condenser microphones. Condenser microphones depend on getting power from a mixer, or preamplifier, to power their output amplifiers and impedance converters (phantom power). Phantom power is DC electric power transmitted through microphone cables to operate the microphone. Condenser microphones are found in a wide variety of physical types. Those types include shotgun, probe style, side-address, lavalier, and head-worn. Their low-mass diaphragms come in a variety of sizes. All you need to know from this is that more power and bigger diaphragms collect more sounds; they are very sensitive. I always tell my students that a good condenser microphone could record a feather hitting the floor (an exaggeration, of course). It is true, however, that if you want to collect the most sound from your sound source, a condenser microphone is the best choice. Good condenser microphones pick up sounds with higher Hertz and are good for recording flutes, violins, and other high-pitched instruments (called high-end responsiveness). Dynamic microphones don't have amplifier circuitry, so they are less sensitive than condensers, and some instruments may not be picked up or sound gets distorted (clipped). Most school groups can get very good recordings using dynamic microphones. One drop of a condenser microphone can damage the diaphragm, and once the diaphragm is damaged, the microphone is shot. Most recording engineers want to use condenser microphones for live recordings, but studio budgets are higher than school budgets, and trained professionals handle the microphones. What you don't want is a subgroup of dynamic microphones known as ribbon microphones. Many of these microphones don't have enough output to attain usable levels for live acoustic recordings.

Should you use microphones for every section?

In a word, no. The tendency of recording into a mixing board is to use all or many of the inputs. It's been my experience, when listening to recordings done this way, that the recordings lose the live feel. Often during mixing, reverb is added and takes away from the acoustic ambience. Why do a live recording if you plan to remove acoustic ambience? Why not take the effort to capture the true character of the performance and preserve what the audience heard? Yes, there are digital effects that can be used to simulate halls of different sizes, and you will get a good finished product if you use them. The problem is, these effects may cause the performance to sound different from the way the performance sounded in a natural acoustic space. This is where the advanced planning I spoke of earlier comes in. Reverb added in the mix can enhance the acoustical sound if the microphones have been well placed (this includes using omni microphones). If you have a particularly weak section you may wish to place overhead microphones in close proximity to the section. Omnidirectional microphones will pick up all sounds but those closest to the microphones will be heard more. This is preferable for me because it maintains the authentic sound.

The problem with planning to use reverb in the mix is that even the best reverb will not be an exact match to the live acoustics of the rehearsal room or concert hall. As I mentioned earlier, carpeted floors, tile floors, cinderblock walls, and sound-treated walls will all yield different sound effects. In professional postproduction, reverb can be added and will yield an authentic live recording sound. Since most schools don't have budgets that will support that, the things discussed in this chapter should be used. Simply put, don't plan to fix it in the mix. There are a lot of things that can be done without depending on the use of EQ (equalization). Try changing the placement of the sound source (move the group forward or backward for natural echo or reverb); change the microphone placement; change the microphone; or try combinations of the things mentioned. Once again, this should all be done before you try the final recording.

In the next chapter I'll be discussing recording during a rehearsal. Recording rehearsals offers an opportunity to get you and your group acclimated to the recording process. The more students record, the less intimidated they will be when recorded during a performance. Performing for an audience is intimidating enough without the added pressure of knowing that every potential mistake will be preserved forever.

Summary

Take the time to plan each step of the recording process and remember to customize everything to your group, equipment, and performance or recording venue. Familiarize yourself with the recording process and all parts of it from production to postproduction. Advanced planning means to write out meticulously each step and make simple diagrams for microphone placement. If others are going to assist you, don't assume they'll know what you want them to do; write everything out clearly.

2

Recording During a Rehearsal in the Rehearsal Room

As stated in chapter 1, one of the most valuable tools for effective teaching is recording your group. Having guided listening exercises for your students to evaluate how well they have executed those items you have worked on in class is a very effective teaching tool. In order to do this, you must have a quality recording to listen to. This chapter will help you to identify specific things that need to be addressed to get an effective recording in a small space and to understand microphone placement and the importance of proximity (how close to the sound source the microphone is). The difference between placement and proximity is that placement refers to the overall position of the microphones and microphone stands; proximity refers to the precise location that collects the most sound (nearness). Having a microphone in the right spot but pointed slightly off-axis or center can mean the difference between a high-quality recording and one that just gets "sounds."

Once again, planning is the most important first step for recording in a rehearsal space. Some of the most important considerations are the following: determining the size of the room; determining how "live" the space will be because of ambience (carpet, tile, treated walls, cinderblock walls, wood floors, etc.); which microphones are best to use based on the group's setup; microphone placement based on overall space; and whether brass and percussion sections need to be repositioned in order to create a more balanced recording. There is no way to get a good recording in a smaller space without addressing these issues and coming up with a plan of attack. If your group is going to be repositioned for recording purposes, you must rehearse them in the new positions so that they may become acclimated to the new placements. What members of the group hear in their new positions will affect their sound, and you as the conductor will need to help them achieve the desired balances. As I've stated before, the best live recordings mirror the best live performances. Listeners to a recording who were present at the live event should hear what they heard live. Listeners who weren't present for the live performance should get the sensation of experiencing the live performance. This is especially important if you are playing back a rehearsal recording to be evaluated by your students. Interestingly enough, you want the rehearsal space to be as dry or flat as possible. You can add effects later that will make the room sound more natural. You can make a dry room sound live, but if the room is too live with echoes, that can't easily be fixed.

Planning ahead will also help you to decide on how you'll deal with room echo caused by tile or cinderblock. Good directional microphones have null points where only the sounds being produced directly in front of them is recorded. Null points are generally the sides or the rear of the microphone. If you don't have good directional microphones or have to use omnidirectional microphones, you may need to put down carpet remnants on tile floors to act as sound dampers. On the walls behind the percussion or brasses you may need to use some kind of dampening materials. Sound shells are generally not good for recordings. They tend to focus the sound outward and can create echoes. Advanced planning and trial and error before doing the main recording will help. It's important that you and your students have time to adjust to anything that is not the norm for sound produced in the rehearsal space. The worst thing you can do is have students come into a drastically changed performance space and expect them to perform in their usual manner, and on top of that, record it. You want your students (and yourself) to be able to feel as natural in a recording setting as possible.

Recording in small rehearsal spaces

Recording in a smaller space can present challenges that recording in a larger space does not, but you can also get a much more focused recording because of lack of air diluting the desired sound. Obviously, the smaller the space, the less room you have for your setup. If you can't move the microphones out, away from the group, the best step is to move the microphones up above the group. This is where using fifteen-foot microphone stands is practical, in most cases using two microphones in an X/Y stereo pattern. Figure 2.1 shows an illustration of X and Y patterns, and Figure 2.2 shows a stereo pair.

This should suffice, but if your group has smaller sections that need to be balanced against larger sections using more microphones will help. Having a working understanding of microphone polar patterns will help you in choosing the right microphones and then deciding on the placement of the microphones.

Here's where knowledge of the three basic microphone types is important: omnidirectional (omni), figure-of-eight (bidirectional), and cardioid (directional). Each one of these types is used to collect the greatest sound possible. A brief description of each of these microphone types will help you to decide which microphone is best for you. Your school budget may not allow you to have different microphones for recording in small spaces and large spaces, so it will be important to understand how each microphone type works in order to decide on which microphones to purchase. If more microphones

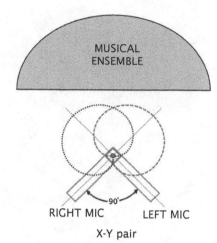

FIGURE 2.1 X/Y setup with 90-degree spacing. Credit Larry Seiler, Los Senderos Studio, LLC, Blanco, TX.

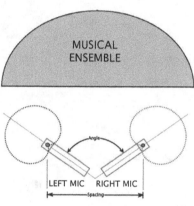

FIGURE 2.2 Near-Coincident Matching Pair 110-degree spacing. Credit Larry Seiler, Los Senderos Studio, LLC, Blanco, TX.

are needed, you'll need to make sure cables are secured to the floor to avoid students tripping over them or disconnecting them accidentally.

Omnidirectional pattern microphones record sounds coming from all directions. Imagine there is a circle of sound, and you want to collect all sounds equally. Figure 2.3 shows an illustration of an omni pair and suggested spacing.

A figure-of-eight pattern will record sounds from the left or right, but there will be a part in the center where sound will not be recorded (this is what the null point mentioned earlier refers to). Figure 2.4 shows two figure-of-eight microphones.

A cardioid pattern microphone has a wide range front and sides, but has a null point in the rear (for our purposes we'll consider the supercardioid and hypercardioid as more focused cardioid patterns). Cardioid microphones derived their name from the heart shape of their pickup pattern. Figure 2.5 shows the cardioid pattern imprinted on the side of the microphone.

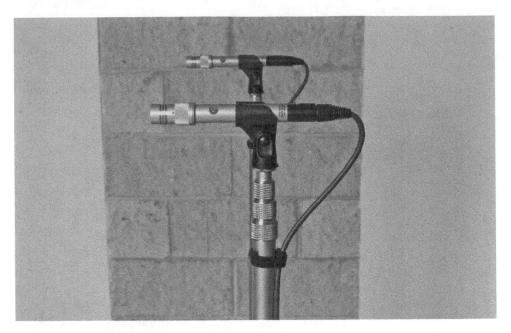

FIGURE 2.3 An omnidirectional pair of microphones. Copyright Shure Incorporated; used with permission.

FIGURE 2.4 Mid-side pair of figure-of-eight microphones. Used by permission of Neumann.Berlin.

This is the pattern that is best used in recording groups when you don't want to pick up ambient sounds, including echoes bouncing off the rehearsal room wall behind the director or conductor's podium. If movement is not a consideration, setting up a hanging omni microphone in conjunction with a stereo pair may be a good choice. Instrumental and vocal sounds travel upward as well as outward, so capturing all of the sounds is useful. Mixing later can help you get a good balance of sounds collected

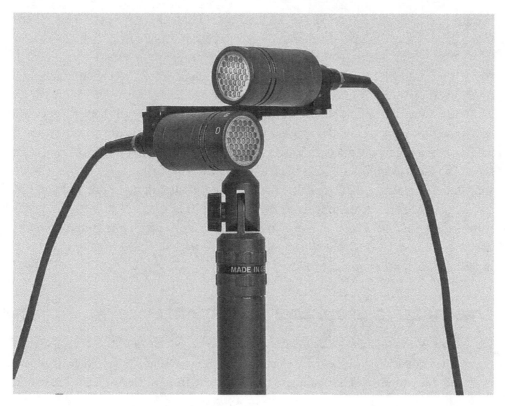

FIGURE 2.5 X/Y matching pair of cardioid microphones on a fifteen-foot stand. Used by permission of Neumann.Berlin.

from all microphones. Having a little air mixed in can enhance the live feel even for a rehearsal. The advantage of using a hanging microphone in a rehearsal space is that there are fewer ambient sounds to worry about (paper rattling, audience coughs and sneezes, etc.). The hanging microphone can be an omnidirectional microphone or a cardioid microphone.

Recording groups that move in a smaller space can be even more challenging; blocking movements (planning or diagramming) so that the group doesn't move beyond the areas where microphones are focused is important. An obvious consideration would be to not have the group move. This solution may help the recording but may not help the group prepare for a future performance. This is another case of how advanced planning will help. It may be that restrictive movement works and that movement won't take the group off-axis (best point for recording).

Microphone placement and proximity

Earlier in this chapter it was mentioned that microphone placement and microphone proximity are important factors in getting a good recording in a small space. Just because the space is small doesn't mean that you will automatically collect all sounds in a balanced way. Directional microphones will collect sounds from the direction in which they are pointed (referred to by recording engineers as "the sonic environment"). If you want to record sounds from three instruments or voices, you should not position a microphone in front of one instrument or voice. This is where proximity comes in. Where should the microphone be placed to record effectively all three parts rather than get an unbalanced sound? Since every space is different because of acoustics, you'll have to keep moving the microphone toward your desired sound sources or away from the sound sources in order to hear which position works best. If you can listen while someone else moves the microphone, the subtle positions can be heard, and you can have them place the microphone in the desired space. This process may seem time-consuming, but time spent here will save lots of time later and help avoid sound dropouts during recording. During your sound check you may want to wear a headset in order to monitor the balance your recording will have.

Overhead microphone placement

For overhead microphone placement in a small space, determine the center spot of the room acoustically. The easiest way is to use a single-sound source (voice, trumpet, etc.), and determine the spot that doesn't have an echo from the left or right; the sound

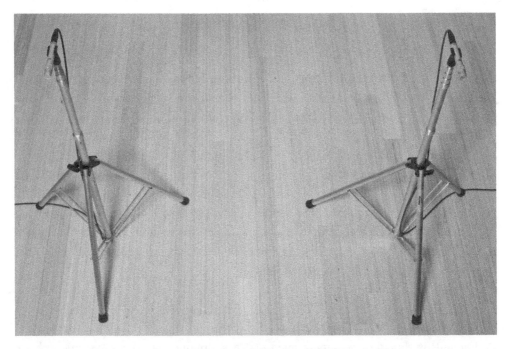

FIGURE 2.6 Matching pair of microphones on individual adjustable fifteen-foot stands able to be spaced wide. Copyright Shure Incorporated; used with permission.

is literally centered. You can easily determine this by standing directly behind or in front of the sound source. You may have seen someone clap in a room to determine the amount of echo and the direction the greatest echo comes from. Once you determine the sound center, hang the microphone five feet above the sound source. This microphone should be an omni microphone that will collect sounds from all sides and center. If natural reverberation (echo) is a problem, you can experiment with raising or lowering the microphone. Technically speaking, reverberation is an echo of an echo (this is referred to as phase differences). Each echo will be weaker than the original sound and can cause a muddy or unclear recorded sound. Your trained ear will recognize this issue immediately. This problem will help you to determine the placement of directional microphones. Figure 2.6 shows directional microphones on adjustable floor stands.

Directional microphone placement

Depending on the size of the sound source, you may or may not need to use an omni microphone. A well-placed stereo pair can collect the desired sounds if placed properly. Placing a pair of microphones seven inches apart or as far as five feet apart on fifteen-foot stands or a close set X/Y pair (Blumlein pair M/S) can get you similar results as an omni

FIGURE 2.7 X/Y matching pairs with 110-degree Y spacing. Used by permission of Neumann.Berlin.

microphone. Place the pair as far behind the conductor's podium as you can. Adjust the angle of the microphones in the direction that covers the widest range. There's not enough space for a stereo image to develop until you're at least six feet from the sound source. If possible, you should be at least ten feet from the sound source before using the X/Y stereo approach (difficult to achieve in most rehearsal rooms but not impossible). Using the stereo pair five feet apart, fifteen feet high can yield a good recording with a cardioid or supercardioid pair (a little more focused cardioid polar pattern). It's important to note that the best stereo images are achieved by having the microphones as close together as possible (crossing the microphones to form an X, close together in parallel position, having them face one another to form a Y, or using a mid-microphone with a bidirectional microphone). There are brackets for these patterns that are attached at the top of the stand. Figure 2.7 shows X/Y matching microphones.

Playback and evaluation: Using the recording as a teaching tool

Because you're an educator and not a professional recording engineer, your focus should be on getting the best possible recording to be used as an educational tool. While you may want to sell recordings or streams as fundraisers, the recording will be best used to archive the achievements of your group and to help the group track its growth. Recording a performance and evaluating it is different from recording a rehearsal. Recording rehearsals at different steps of the learning process will serve to yield a good final performance. The reason it is so important to have good quality recordings of rehearsals and performances is so that your students are able to compare the two. In recording terms, we refer to this as transparency in recording. You want the recording to sound as if the group is performing live during playback. The effect you want is that each listener feels as though he or she is standing in front of the group that is performing and is able to hear the performance clearly. In order to make a good evaluation of the performance (rehearsal or performance), students must be able to hear the good and the bad. They can't critique balance and dynamics if the recording has not been recorded well balanced. You should screen and possibly mix the recording before having the students listen. Once again, imagine having each individual member of the group stand behind you and listen. If each is able to hear what you hear as the director or conductor, the student will be able to make accurate observations.

Once you've gotten a representative recording of your group, you're ready for the formal playback and evaluation component. You should have an evaluation sheet or form for your students guiding them. I always used the forms used for band, orchestra, and choral assessments. This way your students can evaluate how well they have articulated (diction and enunciation for vocalists), effected attacks and releases, phrasing, balance and use of dynamics, and so on. As you go down the sheet before recording, you can evaluate what you need to get on the recording. The stereo image that is presented live should be represented on recordings. This is why engineers who are recording live place stereo microphones 6.78 inches apart if they aren't using an X/Y stereo pattern. Human ears are approximately that distance apart, so the stereo setup mimics what the human ear records. There's no prescribed best way to achieve this, since every small space and large space will be different. Your ear should be the tie-breaker or deciding factor.

Mixing a recording is really no different from what a good director does during a performance. Directors are constantly making adjustments so that the live sound image is good. During mixing and preparing for playback as the mixer you are doing the same thing, except you're manipulating recorded sound. It's actually more difficult as a director because a director only gets one pass. A person mixing can playback over and over and continuously make changes until it's right. You can even have a raw mix for your students to listen to. They can decide on balances and how the stereo image is manipulated. That way you can compare mixing the recording with mixing during a performance. Since most students are technologically savvy, they will surprise you and come to some conclusions on their own. This is all part of using the recording as a teaching tool, and points out the importance of getting a good recording in a rehearsal space.

Summary

Advanced planning is a must. The only way to use a rehearsal recording as a teaching tool is to have a representative recording. Be sure to determine the acoustic strengths and weaknesses of the space. This will determine the number of microphones used, microphone placement, and microphone proximity. You must have an optimal recording for your students to be able to evaluate their performance, individually and collectively. You will also need to turn off the HVAC unit so not to get unwanted noise.

3

Recording in an Auditorium or Large Space

Recording your group in a rehearsal space is an important part of teaching music, but the ultimate goal of performing groups is to perform. Therefore, the best way to evaluate how effective your teaching has been is to record the finished product. This chapter will discuss how to achieve the best recording in an auditorium. Since some schools use a multi-use space for concerts and plays, I'll discuss recording in those spaces in a separate chapter.

Recording in a large space

Some of the things discussed about recording in a small area will also apply to recording in a larger space. There are several techniques that will be unique to recording in auditoriums and large spaces. Older schools have large auditoriums that in most cases are not sonically treated for music performances. They tend to be very loud spaces subject to extreme reverberation. Older buildings used concrete and cinderblock walls and concrete or tile floors (usually concrete, because it is generally more cost-effective). Because of the noise, you may need to turn off the HVAC if it's an older unit. Obviously, you'll need to weigh the known discomfort against the possible noise. It's not impossible to get a good recording in this type of auditorium, but it will be a challenge and will require lots of testing and planning. The same tests that you used in the small room, such as clapping or moving around to find the sweet spot, will work in the auditorium. The difference will be the amount of reverberation in the larger space. It's usually wise to record the sound before it goes to the main part of the auditorium because of the possibility of excess reverberation. That's why having the microphones on the stage, eliminating as much room ambience as possible, is important. These auditoriums may or may not have orchestra pits. As discussed previously, as long as you can set up the microphones six to ten feet away from the sound source, you can get a good stereo image. Most engineers prefer to use M/S technique for these auditoriums.

Schools built in the past twenty years generally have smaller auditoriums that seat no more than six hundred people. Some of these auditoriums have balconies, and some don't. In smaller auditoriums some engineers like to set up a fifteen-foot parallel microphone stand five to ten rows back. Recording in auditoriums such as this can be done with a parallel pair of microphones pointing directly ahead, using the ORTF technique, Decca tree technique, X/Y technique, or mid-side technique. Figure 3.1 shows a parallel pair directly behind the conductor.

The most preferred is the X/Y technique, which uses two cardioid microphones placed at 90-degree angles. The result of this setup is that the microphone on the right picks up the left side of the room, and the microphone on the left picks up the right side of the room. There is a refinement for this technique called the Blumlein pair (M/S), which uses a mid-microphone and a bidirectional microphone. The result of using this technique is that one microphone will pick up the sound source directly, and the bidirectional microphone picks up sounds from the side. The set-up distance is exactly the same as the X/Y except for the fact that you are using a bidirectional microphone. The Blumlein pair is known for creating an exceptionally realistic stereo image, but that image is dependent on the size of the sound source as well as the quality of the room. This setup works best if you have a good-sounding room acoustically to record in, so the smaller auditoriums are better-suited for this technique. Figure 3.2 shows an illustration of the Blumlein pair coverage area.

FIGURE 3.1 Matching pair of Audix SCX25A microphones set up directly behind the conductor's podium. Used by permission of Audix Corporation, Wilsonville, OR.

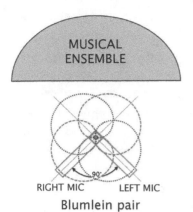

Blumlein pair

FIGURE 3.2 Blumlein pair directional coverage pattern. Credit Larry Seiler, Los Senderos Studio, LLC, Blanco, TX.

Microphone placement and proximity

The M/S technique works well anywhere and does not require a matched pair. You can use a directional microphone with a cardioid pattern along with the bidirectional microphone. The one microphone is bidirectional and uses a figure-of-eight polar pattern. Mid-side is a technique in which both microphones are placed as close as possible to each other, and the stereo image is created by differences in loudness rather than time delays. Figure 3.3 shows a mid-side setup.

Mid-side uses a mid-microphone, which usually has a cardioid pattern, but can also be omni. The mid-microphone is aimed at the source, while a bidirectional microphone (figure-of-eight pattern) is used to pick up sound from the sides. To create a stereo image, the signals have to be decoded by either a mixer or a dedicated decoding plug-in. Several professional engineers use this technique when mixing and postproduction are planned. It sounds more complicated than it actually is.

This technique was patented by Alan Blumlein but was used by Danish Radio for live music broadcasts by Danish Radio engineer Holger Lauridsen, who ushered in its popularity. The advantage of this technique is that once you collect the sounds, you can manipulate them to get the balances you desire to recreate the ultimate live experience you heard during the live performance. Since the stereo image comes from a single microphone in a bidirectional or figure-of-eight pick-up pattern, there is no need for the mid-microphone to be the same model or size. This makes M/S a good choice for programs with limited budgets.

Use of multiple microphones

One of the advantages music directors have over many engineers recording bands, orchestras, choirs, and jazz groups is that music directors work daily on manipulating sound in real time as they conduct. This means that if postproduction is planned, the director's knowledge of the group serves as a good starting point for collecting and

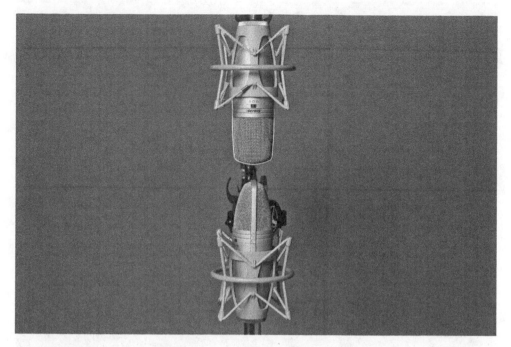

FIGURE 3.3 Mid-side microphone setup. Copyright Shure Incorporated; used with permission.

manipulating the group's sound. Instead of working on the perfect sound, the director is actually working on the sound he or she hears every day. During your preplanning it will be wise to become familiar with the auditorium space that you're using and decide whether an X/Y technique or a mid-side technique (a more refined X/Y) will be best for you. Figure 3.4 shows refined X/Y technique, and Figure 3.5 shows the mid-side coverage.

Another technique used for bands and orchestras is the ORTF technique. The ORTF technique is named for the French radio and television office (Office de Radiodiffusion-Télévision Française). It is a binaural microphone technique designed to imitate the response of your two ears. Two cardioid microphones are placed seven inches apart (the approximate distance between two human ears) at an angle of 110 degrees. An advantage of this technique is that the microphone can be moved around the room until it sounds good to you (as was mentioned in recording in the rehearsal room). You can decide on the best location for the placement based on what you heard when you sound-tested the room.

Another practical and popular technique is the Decca tree. The Decca tree technique is used for recording large bands or orchestras and can work in large or small auditoriums. It uses a special T-shaped microphone stand suspended behind and above the conductor's head. Figure 3.6 shows suggested distances for Decca tree setup.

There are three cardioid microphones, facing left, center, and right. Engineers don't have fixed measurements for this configuration, since it needs to be adjusted based on the size of the group. The microphones are usually placed close together for smaller

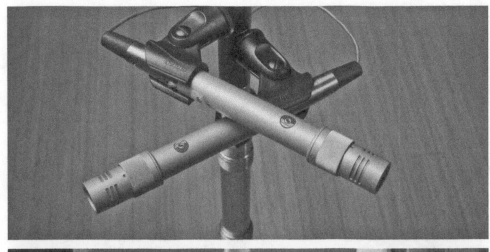

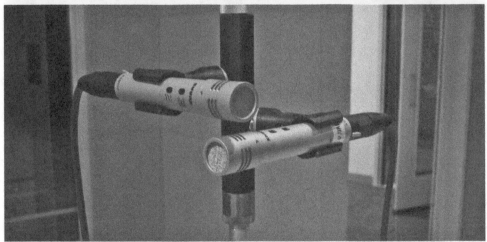

FIGURE 3.4 X/Y close spaced matching microphones. Copyright Shure Incorporated; used with permission.

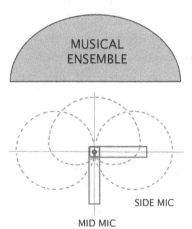

Mid-side technique

FIGURE 3.5 Mid-side set-up diagram. Credit Larry Seiler, Los Senderos Studio, LLC, Blanco, TX.

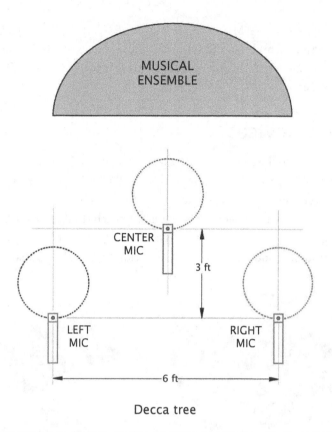

Decca tree

FIGURE 3.6 Decca tree set-up diagram. Credit Larry Seiler, Los Senderos Studio, LLC, Blanco, TX.

groups. The advantage of using this technique in a larger auditorium is that you collect the sound before it gets distorted in any way by the ambient sounds found in larger auditoriums and gives an open sound to smaller auditoriums. In essence, it takes away any negatives that auditorium size may cause.

Which of these techniques you use will be dependent on your personal preferences, budget for microphones and postproduction equipment, the size of your group, and the size of the recording space. Just as with recording in your rehearsal room, recording in an auditorium requires your knowledge of your sound source (group), room constraints (where microphones can and cannot be placed), and whether you plan to use postproduction resources for the finished product. There is no standard choice because no two groups are the same, and no two spaces are the same. Always remember that stereo recording is an attempt to capture what two human ears hear.

One engineer I consulted said that no matter which technique he uses to record the sound source, he always sets up two wireless microphones in the balcony or at the rear of the auditorium to record applause. It's his opinion that fading applause out at the end of each selection adds to the live recording effect. This of course is based on the use of a multichannel mixing board. He also pointed out that when he records guitar ensembles, he prefers to use M/S. The vibrations of strings are best picked up by the mid-microphone aimed at the sound source; as the sound expands, it's picked up by the bidirectional microphone. In his opinion, the only setup not practical for guitar choirs or ensembles is Decca tree.

Hand-held devices

Though not the preferred way to record in an auditorium, hand-held devices have models that replicate X/Y, parallel microphones, and ORTF. Figure 3.7 shows the different microphone patterns on hand-held devices.

Because the distance between microphones is much smaller on hand-held devices, the stereo image will be smaller. If you use a hand-held setup, the best placement would be directly behind the conductor's podium. The closer you are to the sound source, the

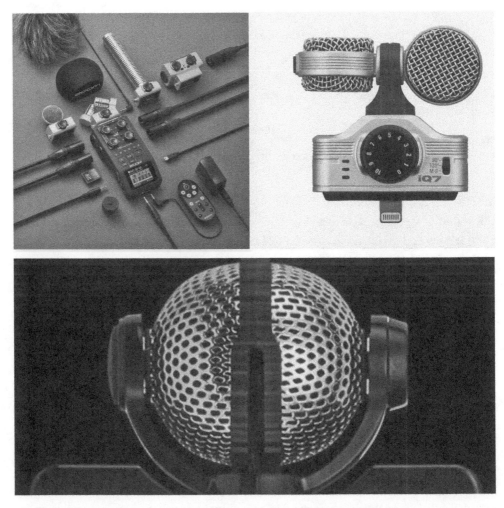

FIGURE 3.7 Zoom hand-held device accessories. Photos used by permission of Zoom, North America.

FIGURE 3.8 Zoom adjustable X/Y microphone. Photos used by permission of Zoom, North America.

better. The second best choice is to mount the device on a fifteen-foot microphone stand and place it five to ten rows back from the stage. The drawback to using this is that as opposed to using microphones, you will record every sound in the vicinity of the device. Figure 3.8 shows the adjustable microphones on the hand-held device.

Summary

Some of the most common mistakes made are from lack of planning and poor judgment. Say that someone has purchased ten microphones and is determined to use all ten of them to record a group of twenty performers. Microphones are aimed at every part of the group and toward the audience to capture applause and audience responses. The result is a recording that even the best postproduction engineers can't fix: you collect every cough, sneeze, program rattle, page turn, and sticky valve. The result is that you can't separate those sounds you want from the sounds you don't want. Using too many microphones can cause you to miss out on capturing a high-quality performance. Advanced planning and having a clear idea of what you want to capture will go a long way to giving you the high-quality recording you desire.

I once had someone record a performance for me, and he came to me after the recording happily reporting that there were places in the music when we were very quiet, so he panned the levels up so that the recording had the same volume throughout. I had left the stage feeling that it was one of that group's best performances, but I have no recording to prove it. Just because there is a soundboard present doesn't mean a soundboard has to be used. Another common mistake is to place microphones too close to parts of the sound source or too close to the whole sound source. That's the equivalent of sitting in front of a trumpet and putting your ear directly in front of the trumpet bell. You will hear much more trumpet than anything else; there will be no possibility of your hearing a balanced sound no matter how the rest of the group is playing. Haphazard microphone placement can ruin even the best planned recording. It is wise for you to supervise microphone placement, and if the sound is going through a soundboard, put on headphones to hear what's being recorded. With two microphone recordings or Decca tree recordings, it's possible to get a good recording that does not have to be mixed.

4

Recording Jazz Ensembles, Show Choirs, and Groups with Amplifiers

One of the biggest challenges of recording jazz ensembles, jazz choirs, show choirs, and other groups that are microphoned with multiple microphones or wireless microphones is collecting amplified sounds and acoustic sounds with a semblance of balance. Most engineers record these groups into a mixing board and then work on balances in post-production. That is the best way, but it is often not the way most groups can record. If you don't have a mixing board, there are still ways to achieve a good recording.

With acoustic groups, recording the sound before it goes out into the large space is preferred but with amplified groups, the only way to get a balanced sound without using a mixing board is to collect the sound after it goes out into the larger space. Placing a Blumlein pair of microphones just offstage or using an X/Y pattern setup five or ten rows back in the center of the auditorium will give you the opportunity to record the sound that is being heard by the audience (some engineers prefer M/S). This means that if you have microphoned soloists singing or playing along with the group, the balance that the audience hears is the same balance that is recorded. One of the best ways to record small groups is to know what you're trying to achieve. That means listening to model groups. Figure 4.1 shows two matching pairs, one in X setup and one in Y setup.

There are multiple sources for listening to good recordings of amateur and professional jazz ensembles and popular jazz choirs or vocal jazz ensembles. Publishers usually have MP3s or other digital recordings and CDs of their songs for you to hear. Most of these recordings were done in studios, but there are several that were done live at venues of various sizes. Don't be deceived by the smaller size of the ensemble; there needs to be the same amount of planning involved with these groups, and the added challenges

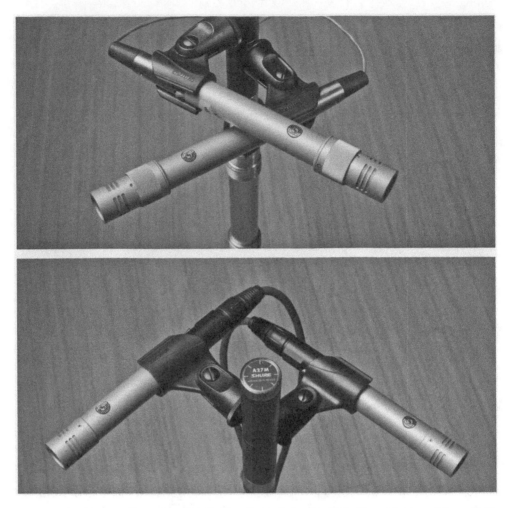

FIGURE 4.1 X/Y microphone setup with bracketed stand tops. Copyright Shure Incorporated; used with permission.

involve movement and the use of electronics. YouTube has plenty of videos for you and your students to watch to get a feel for what you're trying to achieve.

Recording smaller groups

As with recording larger groups, recording smaller groups requires a knowledge of microphone placement and microphone proximity. Since these groups usually have soloists or small groups inside of the small group, you must strive to get a good balance live in order to get a good balance on the recording. Sometimes this means using more microphones, but sometimes it simply means fine-tuning your setup. This is where proximity comes in. During a dress rehearsal, walk around the performance hall and listen to the sounds emitting from the stage. Decide on the kind of balance you'll need going into the "house" while performing live. This is the ultimate sound you want to go on your recording. The microphones can be your ears, and you can decide on which recording style will be best to achieve your desired results.

If you decide to use X/Y recording, it's good to set up the microphones somewhere near the center of the room so that the microphones can pick up the best sounds from the sound source. Figure 4.2 shows an X/Y setup that can be used with a fifteen-foot microphone stand.

Parallel microphone technique and X/Y recording will imitate what your ears hear. Your ears hear in stereo, so your objective is to get the best stereo image possible (that's why the Blumlein pair is so popular). The drawback is that the microphones will pick up ambient sounds as well as performance sounds. Supercardioid microphones or hypercardioid directional microphones will help get a more focused recording but there will still be some unwanted sounds collected.

One of the things about recording a jazz ensemble or a show choir is that microphones are used on individuals. This means that rather than being concerned about recording a stereo recording you can collect as much sound as possible on multiple microphones using a soundboard or mixing board. You can either create balance while

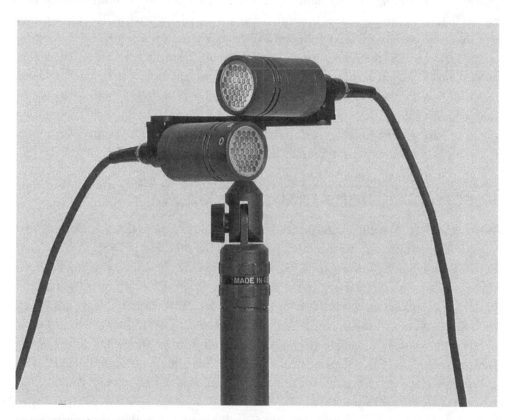

FIGURE 4.2 X/Y (X position) setup with matching cardioid microphone pair. Used by permission of Neumann.Berlin.

FIGURE 4.3 Large mixing board with multiple channels. Photo courtesy of Behringer.

recording or record raw (that is, record everything) and then mix for balance in a studio in postproduction (if possible, try not to make board adjustments during the performance). In this case microphone placement is very important. With show choirs, most of the vocalists are physically microphoned with wireless clip-on or head-worn microphones. The recording is being done through the same board as the house sound. This means that the recording passes through the audio in and out patches. The adjustments you make for balance on the live sound can be exported to the recording for mixing later. Most engineers prefer to import and then export the greatest sound possible. This gives them the opportunity later in postproduction to manipulate the recorded sound in such a way that they're able to get the best possible recording. For this, the use of multiple microphones is an advantage. You have the opportunity to export sounds for recording that aren't affected by the mixing you're doing for the house sound. Figure 4.3 shows a mixing board that can be used for live sound and recording.

Recording groups that move on stage

When recording show choirs and jazz ensembles and other groups that are microphoned you won't necessarily get the flexibility you need to have the best possible stereo sound. Recording everything at the same level will afford you the opportunity to mix better in postproduction. You'll be doing in the studio what you've done during rehearsals and performances except that you'll be using recorded sounds rather than live sounds (when mixing, always be sure to have a safety copy of the recording). With jazz choirs and show choirs, picking up movement is unavoidable. Clip-on microphones will help cancel out some unwanted sounds, but groups that use microphones hanging from the ceiling will collect footfalls and fabric sounds along with voices. Figure 4.4 shows an Audix head-worn microphone wireless system.

If during rehearsals you're satisfied with the sound mix that is going into the house, you can use one of the other live recording techniques (X/Y, Decca tree, M/S, or

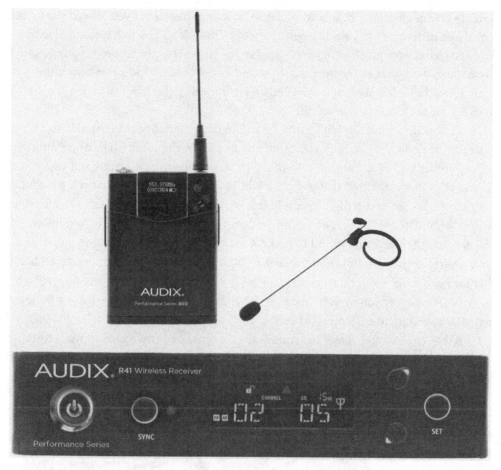

FIGURE 4.4 Audix head-worn wireless microphone system. Used by permission of Audix Corporation, Wilsonville, OR.

parallel). You may even want to do that along with using multimicrophone techniques and compare the sound with what you think the sound mixed through the soundboard will yield. If nothing else, you'll have a recording of the actual performance rather than manipulating recorded sounds to gain the same effect. The live sound mix will determine how good the stereo recording will be, since the soloists and group balances have to be done well (some engineers set up a parallel pair for this purpose). If it's not possible to have a good sound person running the soundboard during setup and sound check, it's best for you to plan to handle everything during the mix.

The natural tendency when recording small groups is to try to force a natural sound by compensating with the use of more microphones. As I've pointed out, recording small groups that are stationary is no different from recording large groups that are stationary. The only difference is that with a smaller sound source, the output won't be as great (in terms of volume). If you run electronic instruments through the soundboard, you lessen the chances of signal losses and have more control over the signal quality (use of effects). A simple accessory such as a splitter allows you to send the signal from one instrument to two different channels. This allows you to have someone mixing live sound without affecting the output of the channel to the recorded sound patch. Remember, you want to record as much sound as possible, and you don't want the volume to fluctuate because someone is raising or lowering the input in order to achieve balance for the house or live sound.

In the chapter on mixing boards I'll talk in detail about board channels and their uses, but for now it's just important that you know your options when using multiple microphones and external sound sources. The issue of acoustic sound and electronic sound becomes something that you must address while mixing. How do you get sound that has air in it to match digital sound? This issue is extremely important when mixing voices with instruments that are recorded directly into the soundboard. You'll have to manipulate the electronic sound to make it match live sound. The mixing board gives you several options on how to achieve this. I'll be discussing this in more detail later, but for now, understand that a good soundboard will have effects that will allow you to alter or refine every sound that's recorded on that particular channel. Figure 4.5 shows a digital soundboard with preset affects.

Show choirs often have instrumental accompaniment which means recording instruments and voices together. Recorded properly, the voice simply becomes another instrument. The same is true with vocal soloists with jazz ensembles. You want to record

FIGURE 4.5 Digital mixing board with presets. Photo courtesy of Behringer.

the voices at the highest import level possible. When mixing, you just balance the recorded voices with the recorded instruments. Mixing the live sound is much more of a challenge than collecting the recorded sound. Your only concern is selecting a microphone that records voices well.

One of the biggest mistakes is to have soloists moving around singing with handheld microphones. As the students move, there's a possibility of feedback and dropoffs. Simply put, you'll hear sound distortion and squeaks coming through. Once this happens, your recording is ruined. If you can't have wireless clip-on microphones or head-worn microphones, use omni microphones hanging near the areas where the soloists will be singing and block your movements accordingly. Cardioid and supercardioid

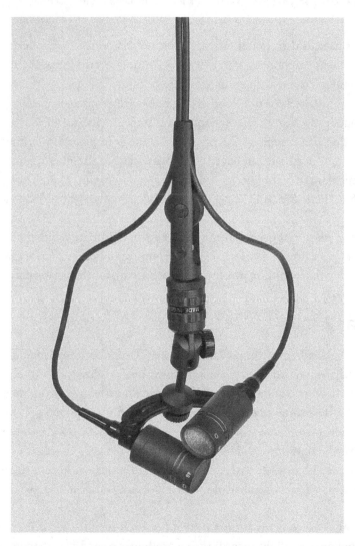

FIGURE 4.6 X pattern cardioid matching pair on a ceiling microphone stand. Used by permission of Neumann.Berlin.

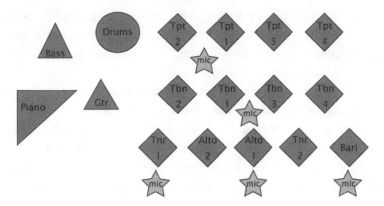

FIGURE 4.7 Basic jazz ensemble setup with stars indicating microphone placement.

microphones used as directional microphones will also work. The soloists will need to know where the microphones are so that they can sing toward them. Figure 4.6 shows a pair of cardioid microphone hanging from the ceiling.

Another mistake is to use floor microphones (microphones placed on the floor). Floor microphones will record every sound on stage, including all footfalls and other movements. For jazz ensembles the biggest mistake is to place a solo microphone too close to a section. It's better to have the soloists walk to the microphone rather than record an unbalanced sound because of microphone proximity. Figure 4.7 shows mic placement for a basic big band setup with one microphone for trombone and trumpet soloists.

Common sense and good planning will help to eliminate some of these problems. It's wise to record a dress rehearsal of small groups in the performance space. This way you can practice the recording process while practicing for the performance.

Summary

Planning is the single most important first step. Use your knowledge of past performances to help you decide where the strengths and weaknesses of the output of the sound source will be. Not only will this determine how many microphones you'll use, but it will also determine microphone placement and microphone proximity, the two most important microphone issues. If your vocalists are wearing clip-on or head-worn microphones, you'll want to avoid movements that will cause cancellation or feedback. Once a signal is lost or distorted, there's nothing that can restore it during the mixing process. This simply means avoid floor monitors and speakers as you block their movement.

If you must place microphones in front of each section, be careful to use directional microphones for tight recording (microphones aimed at a specific source). You don't want sounds from one microphone bleeding into another microphone. During mixing you won't be able to isolate particular sounds if they are on two different channels. This only matters if you're going to adjust balances during mixing. This is a very important detail if you want to give yourself options and flexibility during postproduction. Managing the group's output balance once you've placed the microphones will make it unnecessary to use multiple microphones. Jazz ensembles generally don't need individual sections microphoned unless they have balance problems. The saxophone section may need microphones for sound reinforcement to balance with the brasses, but microphones generally don't need to be used for brasses. Microphones are usually used for soloists only. If you have someone working the board, avoid having him make any adjustments during the performance. Record everything and mix after the performance. Recording smaller groups is in many ways the same as recording larger groups.

5

Recording Away from School

Performing in your school can be challenging, and trying to record away from your school can be quite overwhelming if you haven't given it a lot of forethought. Since no two performance venues are the same, you should try to contact someone who is familiar with the venue that you will be performing in for your recording to find out what kind of setup would be best. If it's not possible for you to actually visit the location, it will be important for you to find out about dead zones or places that are not acoustically sound. Dead spots or dead zones are places where reverberation does not happen naturally. In order to get the best possible recording, you must know where and how to set up your microphones. The same tests that you used at your school, clapping to hear how the room responds and walking around to find the sweet spot, will work. If you're going to use an omnidirectional microphone, cover one ear and listen with the other to find the sweet spot in order to correctly place the microphone. Remember, you can't decide where to place the microphone by sight alone. Don't make the mistake of assuming the microphone should be placed dead center of the recording space without performing basic sound tests. You may also discover that a parallel pair may need to have more space between them than at your home venue.

Since in most cases you will be with your group, you may need to have someone who is familiar with recording setup to do a sound check for you. If you don't have someone who can do this, choose a warmup or scales your group can do without your conducting, so that you can walk around the performance space and determine the best places to set up your microphones.

Recording away from your school means trying to adjust quickly to an unfamiliar space and overcome the anxiety of trying to adjust on the spot. To some degree, you must expect the unexpected. The best way to record in an unfamiliar space is to take the space out of the equation. Set up a pair of microphones behind the director to capture the sound before it's exposed to the acoustics of the unfamiliar room. A stereo pair, X/Y setup, or mid-side is the easiest to set up and get a good recording. In some cases, hand-held devices may be your best and most practical option. However, a drawback of

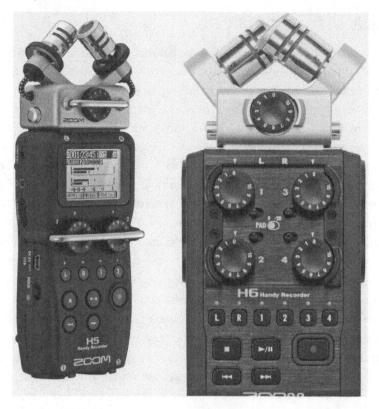

FIGURE 5.1 Zoom hand-held devices. Photos used by permission of Zoom, North America.

hand-held devices is that lower-end equipment will not have good high-end responsiveness, so high-pitched instruments may not record well. For choral groups this won't be an issue, so hand-held devices would be your best choice, especially if there is movement involved. Figure 5.1 shows a Zoom hand-held unit.

Recording in an unfamiliar space

Even though you may be recording in an unfamiliar space, there will be certain things about the stage and the dimensions that will be similar to your location. When planning, it would be wise to start with those things that are similar or the same. Once you have started with the familiar, you can start to evaluate the differences. Using a parallel pair setup directly behind the podium will probably be the best plan if you have no idea of the dimensions of the auditorium. This setup will help you to collect the most from the sound source without losing much of the sound produced. For larger groups the Decca tree setup directly behind the podium would be ideal, because the microphones would cover the whole stage from all directions not as an omni microphone but as three-directional microphones, each recording a specific segment of the stage. Some engineers like to use mid-side to get a good stereo image.

Use of a stereo pair only

There are two ways that you will be using the parallel pair. The first would be to set up directly behind the conductor. As stated before, this is the most preferred. You could also set up five rows back in the auditorium. Keep in mind the microphones will record ambient sounds as well as sounds from the sound source. Because of this, you will need to take care in your setup. Using a hypercardioid pair or supercardioid pair would be best for the setup. Hypercardioid microphones are good directional microphones that can be directed at the sound source and eliminate many unwanted sounds. Their polar pattern is a bit more narrow than the supercardioid microphones. The X/Y pattern is good when using matching supercardioid or hypercardioid microphones. The microphones should be placed on a fifteen-foot stand seven inches apart in order to achieve a good stereo image as a parallel pair imitating human ears. Most of the ambient sounds from below the microphones will be cancelled by the dominant sounds coming from the sound source. There are engineers who advise using omni microphones in unfamiliar venues because they record the widest range by collecting sounds from all directions. If your group is balanced and uses a compact setup, omni microphones are your best choice. These microphones are like your ears; they hear every sound and react to the most dominant sounds. The Blumlein pair produces a very realistic stereo image, but the quality of recordings is dependent on the acoustics of the room and the size of the sound source. This was discussed earlier and is one of the most widely used setups for remote recordings (that is, recordings done away from a studio). Figure 5.2 shows the coverage area of the Blumlein pair.

Other than using a Blumlein pair, a parallel pair of omni microphones is also an effective choice. If you're not going to be mixing multitracks, there are very few drawbacks to using omni microphones. This is because omni microphones will collect sounds from all directions on stage. If you use hand-held devices, you're essentially using hand-held omni microphones because they're designed to collect every dominant sound.

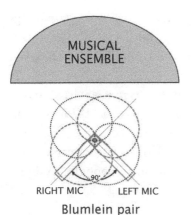

Blumlein pair

FIGURE 5.2 Blumlein pair diagram. Credit Larry Seiler, Los Senderos Studio, LLC, Blanco, TX.

Making adjustments for the unexpected

Every recording engineer will tell you that you need to be prepared for the unexpected. You must anticipate every need before every potential circumstance that will negatively impact your recording. My motto has always been "be prepared, and you won't panic." If you have any time for advanced planning, you should perform the clap test to check out the acoustics in the room (clap to see where you get the most or least echo). That, along with your ear test (using your ears to find the sweet spot) will help you determine where to set up the microphones. If you have a hand-held device on a stand, you'll have a very easy setup without wires or the need for a soundboard. The drawback is that the sound you record will most likely be the sound you get. Most hand-held devices can be used with software like Cubase that will give you some opportunities to mix if you record in waveform audio file format (WAV) format (up to eight tracks), or you can use a digital mixer. Figure 5.3 shows a hand-held device being used with a laptop.

The unexpected is just that: things you don't know will happen. Advanced planning will help reduce the number of problems you may face. Simple things such as adjusting your group's setup in order to give you greater control over the output from the sound source will help. You may not be familiar with the acoustics of the venue, but you are very familiar with your group's output. If you're able to do a sound check,

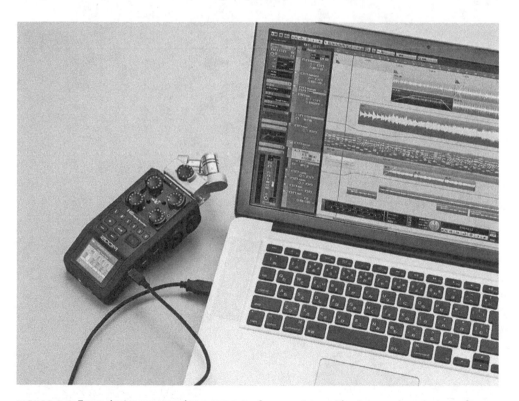

FIGURE 5.3 Zoom device connected to a computer for use mixing with mixing and mastering software. Photos used by permission of Zoom, North America.

experiment with how closely compacted your group needs to be or how expanded they need to be. Try to use setups that you're used to and that your students will be able to adjust to on the spot. Place the microphones based on the group's output, where your ears tell you that you can pick up the most sound, and where the type of microphones you're using will work best.

It's wise not to plan on using an unfamiliar soundboard. True, all soundboards have basically the same channel strips, and it's just a question of the number of channels the board has; the unknown is how the effects will differ. You may be able to adjust quickly and easily, but you can't afford to take a chance unless you know that you have time to set up the board prior to your performance. As a director, you don't need this headache. A parallel pair or one or two hand-held devices will suffice. Your priority should be to have your group ready to perform at the highest level and to be able to record the performance without doing anything that will be a distraction. This is why it's best if possible to have someone else work a soundboard for a sound check. If you can have a student conductor lead the group while you check for the best places to put the microphones, that would be great. That way you get to hear the group and adjust microphone proximity or microphone placement in general.

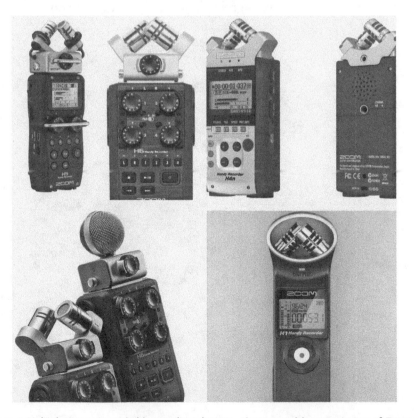

FIGURE 5.4 Multiple Zoom hand-held recording devices. Photos used by permission of Zoom, North America.

The thing that's most important to the success of a recording in an unfamiliar place is to make sure your group can have a good performance. There is no need to have a good recording setup if your group is not ready to give a good performance. Fortunately, preparing your group and setting up for a good recording can be combined. If you're doing a warmup for your group, take note of the sonics of the venue or space. Listen carefully for dead spots or places that are too "live." Set the microphones in places to avoid or compensate for these problems. Fewer microphones are generally the best solution. One of the advantages of using a hand-held device is that you can hold it during your warmup and move about so that you can see by the meter where you're getting the strongest signal. You can either set up your microphones there or place the hand-held device on a stand and record with it. You can even record with both and listen later to decide which recording was better. Should you decide to mix later, you have the option of using both recordings by running the hand-held device through the mixing board. The point is to use your time wisely and focus your attention on getting the best performance that will yield a good recording. Figure 5.4 shows hand-held devices that can be used for remote recording away from your school.

Summary

Plan ahead. If you're recording at another school, consult the director or someone at the school who is familiar with the recording space to get information you'll need to plan your recording.

Adjust your arrival time to give yourself time to explore the unfamiliar space. No matter how much advanced information you get, personal experience in the space is a must.

Carry as little equipment as possible. Don't allow set-up time and recording planning to impact your performance negatively. Remember, a good performance is the priority. To cut down on time, decide whether hand-held devices can yield the best results for you without compromising your recording. Do whatever you can to save time and energy.

6

Recording in Areas That Are Not Acoustically Treated

At some point, you may decide that you want to record outside or in areas that are not acoustically treated. Getting a good recording under these circumstances may be difficult, but will still be a priority for you. This chapter is designed to make you aware of the challenges and also to offer you some suggestions on how to get a good recording under less-than-perfect conditions. Recording outside, in gyms, or in gymtoriums (a gym with a stage in some older buildings) can create similar challenges and therefore can have similar solutions.

Recording outside performances

Recording outside presents a myriad of problems. Obviously, there are many sounds that can't be eliminated, but microphoning and microphone placement can greatly reduce them. Depending on the location, traffic sounds, sounds of nature (birds, dogs barking, etc.), wind, airplanes, and people all present great challenges. So how can you deal with this before postproduction? Microphone choices, microphone placement, and microphone proximity are important. The idea is to collect the sounds from the target sound source before it gets distorted by ambient noise.

Before discussing the best way to record outside, let's look at what not to do when recording outside. If recording inside, you want to set up two stereo microphones behind the conductor on a fifteen-foot microphone stand; outside you don't want that kind of distance between the microphones and the sound source. The more space you have between the sound source and the microphones, the more unwanted sounds will be recorded. Also, since sound travels upward as well as outward, much of what you want to record may not be recordable. Even the best mixing and mastering can't fix a recording that is filled with unwanted ambient sounds. Remember, the idea of recording is to capture the best recording you can. Whether the recording is for an outside commencement ceremony or a football game, the same setups can be used.

Some microphone placement may be limited based on what's being recorded. If you're recording a marching band, you're literally trying to hit a moving target. A stationary band or choir can be "microphoned tight." This means placing the microphones as close to the sound source as possible. This is one time you don't want air to mix with the sound, since there's little or no natural reverberation. Any reverberation you get outside will be in the form of a delay or phase shift. Some engineers prefer recording mono rather than stereo outside because of the difficulty of getting a good stereo image.

Recording outside is a case where some engineers prefer the M/S setup over X/Y and other stereo setups (for stationary groups). M/S recording gives you a little more control over the stereo image than you have with X/Y. M/S doesn't work well with marching bands, because you can't move the microphones along the sidelines or field with the band (unless you're using wireless microphones and can roll them). In the case of stationary bands, orchestras, or choirs, a parallel pair a distance apart will work. Most engineers choose not to use X/Y microphoning outside but some get very good recordings by placing the microphones in front of the conductor directly in front of and close to the stationary sound source. Having a microphone overhead is not always practical or possible. A strong wind can distort the sound and possibly cause injury if blown down. The parallel pair setup makes it possible for the microphones to be hand-held. You can get a good recording outside, but not as good as one done with the help of walls to block out unwanted noise or capture the most sound from your sound source. Noise is an unavoidable problem when recording outside, so choosing microphones that have null points that will cancel out unwanted sounds is important. Figure-of-eight microphones are preferred in order to do this. These microphones, when placed directly in front of the sound source, will collect the most prominent sounds and cancel sounds that are of lower decibel levels. Figure-of-eight recording is much better than using omni microphones outside. Figure 6.1 shows a figure-of-eight pair.

Omni microphones are "pressure microphones," meaning that they record sound from all directions based on the pressure on the microphone's diaphragm. Wind can distort what's being recorded because of the pressure from the wind hitting the diaphragm (a wind screen or microphone cover can help reduce the wind effect). Rather than responding directly to pressure, the microphone responds to the difference in pressure between the front and the rear of the diaphragm. Omni microphones are pressure microphones because they respond to pressure, and figure-of-eight microphones are known as "pressure gradient" microphones because they detect the velocity of sound waves. This means that the wind does not hit the diaphragm directly, so sound from the sound source is more dominant. The microphone is very sensitive to sounds approaching from either the front or rear axis, but sounds approaching from the side cause no ribbon movement at all (a null point). What this means for you is that sounds from the sound source will cancel ambient sounds since sounds off-axis will not be picked up as

FIGURE 6.1 Mid-side setup with a matching pair in figure-of-eight setup. Used by permission of Neumann.Berlin.

dominant sounds. There will obviously be some unwanted sounds collected, but they give your recording the impression of a live performance. Wind shields and microphone covers will help cut down on most of the distortion caused by wind.

Because of cords and accessibility to power outlets, a soundboard may not be practical outside. If there is a press box in your stadium, you may be able to set up a small soundboard there. Your preplanning will help you decide if that's practical. Should you decide to use a soundboard, you'll have to use wireless microphones. Using wireless microphones presents the problem of drop-outs: the signal being dropped or interference creating distortion. Because you can't use cables on a football field, if you choose to use microphones you really don't have a choice other than wireless. Schools that have successful football teams tend to have good sound systems for announcing the game's play-by-play. This may give you access to a good soundboard in the press box and external electrical outlets or extension cords. For digital recording, there is another option outside—hand-held digital recording devices. There are wireless devices that use Wi-Fi that are perfect for use outside. These devices can be used with wireless digital mixers.

Hand-held devices

Sometimes the use of hand-held devices is the most practical way of recording in situations where the use of microphones or access to electrical outlets is not possible. Zoom hand-held devices can be used as stand-alone devices or can be used with digital mixers. Zoom also has microphones that can be attached to iPhones, iPads, and Android tablets. These hand-held devices can be used with digital mixers like the Zoom digital mixer or Behringer digital mixers with Wi-Fi. Figure 6.2 shows Zoom attachments and Wi-Fi digital mixers.

Lower-level hand-held devices may not record higher-pitched instruments without distortion or clipping the sound, but if you're recording outside it won't really matter because you'll lose those instruments even with the best microphones. There have been advancements in digital technology that can give you a high-quality recording without a noticeable drop off from recording with microphones and a soundboard. Hand-held recording devices record with an X/Y configuration that can be adjusted to yield a recording of a complete sound source or a parallel microphone pattern. Some hand-held devices can be used with wireless systems and Bluetooth, and can interface with soundboards that can pair with them. Newer models have their own multichannel digital mixers. These mixers can record up to eight tracks when the WAV option is selected or two tracks when MP3 is selected. Figure 6.3 shows a Zoom digital mixer.

With hand-held devices you are not limited to the use of a single device, nor are you limited to using them in a fixed location. If the sound source moves, so can the hand-held device. Using hand-held devices is the best way to record in multiuse facilities, gyms, and outside. It is also the simplest way to record in an unfamiliar venue. The biggest problem you will encounter is the recording of ambient sounds. The null points of a hand-held device are not the same as a microphone pair, because of the size of the

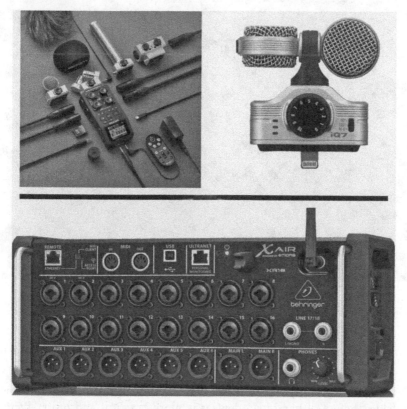

FIGURE 6.2 Wireless hand-held with attachments and wireless Wi-Fi stereo mixer. Photos used by permission of Zoom, North America and courtesy of Behringer.

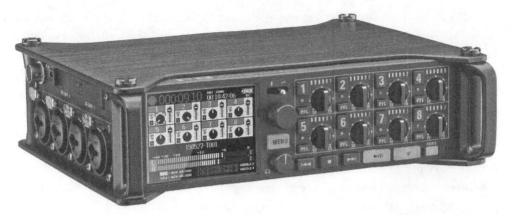

FIGURE 6.3 Eight-track digital mixer for hand-held devices. Photo used by permission of Zoom, North America.

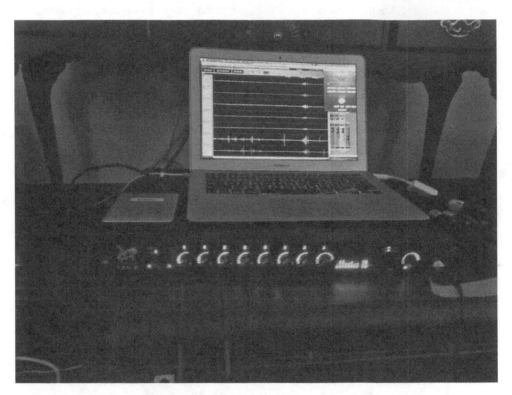

FIGURE 6.4 Computer program in use with a mix from a hand-held device. Photo courtesy of Mike Monseur, Bias Mastering Studio, Springfield, VA.

device and the distance between the built-in microphones. Even though you can adjust the space between microphones, you're talking millimeters rather than feet. Even with that, you can compensate by simply getting as close to the sound source as possible.

Outside, the use of hand-held devices is more practical and more efficient than using wireless microphones. The issue of dropouts is eliminated because the devices are self-contained. The tracks being recorded are stored on the device or on a digital disk. Some soundboards can take these disks, or the device can be connected to the soundboard to transfer the data. From that point the mixing process is the same as having been recorded with microphones. There is available software that allows you to download and mix your recording on your computer. Figure 6.4 shows a computer program in use with a mix from a hand-held device.

Recording in poorly treated areas

As with recording outside, recording in poorly treated areas can be a challenge. If you have a chance to test the acoustics, you may have all of the options discussed thus far at your disposal. The biggest difference between recording inside with poor sound treatments and recording outside is that inside you will have too much reverberation. Your setup and microphone choice will need to compensate for this. This is another case of tight microphoning to get the sounds from the sound source before they get distorted. You will need to find the sweet spot and place the microphones in such a way that echoes will hit the microphones' null points.

If you have access to electrical outlets and can use a soundboard, wired or wireless microphones can be used. If you don't have access to electrical outlets or time to set up and test the acoustics, use hand-held devices. These devices can also be set up on microphone stands. Since they are set up as a stereo pair (built-in), all you may need is one fifteen-foot microphone stand. Setup takes hardly any time, and all you need to do is find the sweet spot to get a good recording.

Summary

There are many things to avoid or not do. Outside, do not use wires for power or to connect to a soundboard. Besides the possibility of someone tripping over the wires, there's the probability that wires will be disconnected by people walking around the recording area. Do not set up microphone stands that can be blown over or knocked down, causing injury. If possible, do not set up microphones on the fifty-yard line if the band is moving away from the fifty; your sound source will move off-axis, and you'll get an uneven recording. Do not plan to have a great deal of electronic equipment outside in case of rain or other forms of precipitation. Do not use multiple omni microphones outside. Directional microphones are better. Do not set up microphones more than ten feet from the stationary sound source. Sound waves expand outward, and diminish with distance. Imagine sound waves as ripples in water if you drop a pebble into the water. The closer you are to the source, the more concentrated the ripples are. The farther you are from the sound source, the weaker the vibrations are, so the sound collected will not be as strong. Do not stand near the audience with wireless microphones or hand-held devices. You'll record every cheer or catcall, but very little of your intended sound

FIGURE 6.5 Hand-held units with X/Y and omni microphone attachments. Photo used by permission of Zoom, North America.

source. Remember, microphones of all kinds record the strongest sounds in their proximity. The quality of the recording done outside with hand-held devices may not be as good as a recording done inside with quality microphones, but because of the advancements in digital technology and the use of Wi-Fi, it is possible to get a high-quality recording. Figure 6.5 shows the kinds of hand-held devices available for use outside.

7

Mixing a Performance Recording

If you decide to use multiple microphones or plan to record through a mixing board (soundboard), there are a few things you need to know. If it's possible to get a professional sound person to come in and record your group using a soundboard for sound reinforcement or live recording, that's probably your best choice. If you decide to do it yourself, have a soundboard or a picture of a soundboard near while reading this section. The size of the soundboard doesn't really matter because the basic functions are the same regardless of size. It's not my intent to furnish information for the recording hobbyist or turn you into an engineer; things discussed in this chapter are purely to help you mix your recording. Figure 7.1 shows the inside of a studio control room.

What is a mixer or soundboard?

A mixer basically combines a selection of inputs into a few outputs, thus "mixing" the inputted sounds. All mixers will have at least a volume control on the output. Most will have volume or level controls on each input, also known as channels. Many mixers will have a variety of control knobs on each channel, from gains or trims to EQ and auxiliaries and buses (a path in which you can route audio signals to a particular destination). The mixers I'll be discussing have at least ten channels (inputs) or more. Most moderate-to-large consoles fit into this category (large boards have at least twenty-four tracks). Figure 7.2 shows a soundboard layout.

Mixers or soundboards are very important for multimicrophone recording, and before you set up and record, you should check your settings with a run-through or sound check. Most people don't realize the importance of a sound check. I like to refer to them as a "house balance" check because when using a mixer, you can get the best

FIGURE 7.1 Full sized recording console inside a recording studio. Photo courtesy of Bias Recording Studios, Springfield, VA.

FIGURE 7.2 Large mixing board. Photo courtesy of Behringer.

balance possible before recording the first song. Let's take a look at the parts of a mixer. Figure 7.3 shows a soundboard with multiple tracks.

The purpose of the knobs is to adjust the quality of sound each microphone is recording. You want to "trim" the sound so that the timbre of each instrument or voice

FIGURE 7.3 Digital mixer with presets. Photo courtesy of Behringer.

is an accurate depiction of what those instruments or voices sound like when they are not amplified. Each strip has multiple knobs that allow you to tweak the sound to adjust high, mid, and low frequencies to come up with the timbre you hear as the characteristic sound of a particular voice or instrument. You want to shape the sound during the sound check (not during the performance). There's nothing like hearing sound characteristics change because someone was adjusting knobs during the performance.

When using a mixer, all gains and trims should be set before the actual performance begins. Analog mixers need this done manually, and digital mixers can be preset to do this (in the next section I'll discuss analog and digital mixers in detail).

The most important thing to understand about mixers is understanding the channels. On almost all consoles the signal comes in physically through the back of the device; the channels are laid out in straight-line strips (channel strips). The signal passes through that channel's various controls from top to bottom, with the gain or trim at the top and the fader at the bottom. The gain will control the amount of input for a channel. The fader will adjust the output of that particular strip after all of the gain, trim, and shaping have been done. Each of these strips contributes to the finished product of the channel after the sound is input from the microphone or external device. A master fader will control the output of all of the channels mixed together with added effects such as reverb.

Analog and digital mixers

There are two basic types of mixers: analog and digital. Analog mixers process the original signals internally in their analog form, and the signals can be converted to a digital form. Digital mixers convert analog signals into digital forms, and much more can be done with the signal. Digital mixers are resistant to noise, are smaller, and can be expanded. Analog mixers are generally easier to learn to use than digital mixers. They have meters that are easy to read because you will see a needle that shows the input level for each channel. If the needle goes into the red zone, you can see (as well as hear) that the sound is distorted. The control layout follows the signal's flow and is therefore easy to see and understand. Analog mixers are generally less expensive than digital mixers. If you only need a few channels with a basic set of effects and features, a simple analog mixer is the most economical choice; if you look at Appendix B, you'll notice the lower prices from all manufacturers. Digital mixers

FIGURE 7.4 Digital mixer with multiple-channels. Photo courtesy of Behringer.

are a bit more complex. They have settings that can be preprogrammed, mixing and processing functions can be set so that you don't manually have to follow the signal or watch the input meters, you can expand and use external devices, they're noise-resistant, and they have multiple functions in small spaces. Because hand-held units and microphones can be used at the same time and run through a digital mixer, digital mixers are very practical for school use. Digital mixers require more training for use than analog mixers, so there will be a smaller pool of users in a school setting. Figure 7.4 shows a digital mixer.

Starting the mixing process

One of the first things you want to do before starting the mixing process is to make a backup copy of the original recording. Using a mixing board in postproduction is not that different from using it during recording, except that rather than using live sound, you're using recorded sound. This is where the various effects come into use. One of the things that happens as you progress from small boards to large boards is the number of effects knobs you'll have for fine-tuning your sound. Each of these effects will be used to create a polished recording. Think of a diamond in the rough: you chip away unwanted parts of the diamond so that you can get to the valuable part inside. At first you chip away chunks, but as you get closer to the pure diamond, you work more delicately. Comparatively, in order to chip away and polish sound, you must have the highest quantity of signal possible to yield the highest quality of sound possible (that's how gain differs from volume). Each channel needs to have the recorded sound as strong as possible without any distortion. If the signal is clipped because the input is too strong, the sound is canceled. Figure 7.5 shows a close-up view of the channel strip knobs.

FIGURE 7.5 Analog mixer focusing on channel knobs. Photo courtesy of Behringer.

This is why condenser microphones are preferable; they don't clip at higher Hertz levels. You cannot recover sounds that are clipped or distorted. This is where microphone proximity is important also. A microphone set too close will clip or distort if overloaded. No matter what you try to do to trim the recorded sound, any sound that has been clipped or distorted cannot be balanced with other recorded sounds. Balancing and mixing a recording starts with microphone placement and microphone proximity. Yes, you will be able to overcome some issues in postproduction, but you'll be settling for what you have to work with. Ideally, you want to start your mix with the best recorded sounds possible on all channels.

Getting the right balances to keep the live performance feel

During a live performance nobody should be using the mixing board to adjust the sound that will be used for the recording. Tracks that are collected to be used for the recording should be recorded at the highest gain level that does not clip or distort. This is called gain-staging or gain-structuring. Gain controls the quantity of the sound coming into the channel, not the volume going out (faders control output volume). Use the outputs for your recording (auxiliary out or aux out), and your live sound should be different. Aux outs are generally used for monitors for the live sound. If the board is being used for house or live sound, the auxes used should not be used to send the recorded sound out. This is why most soundboards have multiple outs. You can assign the outs that go to the live sound and at least two buses that feed the sound collected for the recording. This has nothing to do with the number of microphones being used, since multiple channels can feed a single out. Figure 7.6 shows auxiliary knobs.

The best way to get good balances when mixing your recording is to be sure you collect the most sound from your sound source as possible. This means getting the

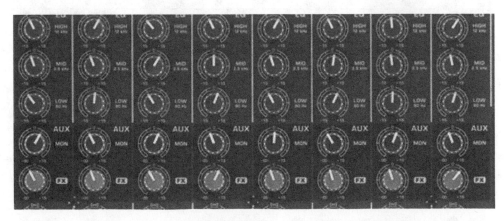

FIGURE 7.6 Analog mixer focusing on auxiliary knobs. Photo courtesy of Behringer.

highest levels on all channels without distortion. When sending the signals to output, push the fader up to the highest output levels you can get without distortion. Ideally, you want to have a flat (dry without reverb) signal to work with as you attempt to mix all of your channels. This way you are recreating live-performance conditions. The reason you don't want the outs that are feeding the recording to feed the house or live sound is that you want the maximum signal going to the recording, and that would be too loud and unbalanced for anyone listening live. By mixing, you can adjust the balances for the recording. Getting balances during mixing is no different from getting balances during a performance. It's actually easier to get a good mix from a recording since you get to have as many passes as needed as opposed to the one pass you get while conducting a live performance. As I've mentioned previously, this is where you as the director have an advantage over a professional engineer. You work on balances while conducting every day. Your familiarity with the sound source makes achieving the ideal balance possible. You should remember, however, that if you want to raise or lower balances within the sound source, you must use several microphones on separate channels. If you can't control the input, you can't control the output. If two sections are recorded by a single microphone on a single channel, you can't adjust the volume or balance within that single track. If you know your clarinet section has a weak live output, you'll need to microphone them with a directional microphone if you want to tweak their sound in the final mix. It's better to microphone soloists and sections and discover that you didn't need to do so, than to not microphone them and discover after the fact that you should have done so. You'll want to devote a single channel to any voice or section you think you'll need to raise or lower in its channel's output.

Once you've mixed, you can add reverb and other effects to the finished product. In most cases the purpose of reverb is to create the feel of natural echo in a live hall. Most soundboards allow you to adjust the reverb and other effects for each channel. The larger boards, like the ones in professional studios, give you a wider array of effects. Most of the added knobs are for equalization (EQ). There are digital software effects that can be downloaded onto your computer for mixing or mastering if your budget doesn't support off-site mixing or mastering. Some of these software programs have a selection of reverb effects that simulate different hall sizes.

Using a mixing board in postproduction

Using a mixing board in postproduction after mixing has been completed is commonly known as the mastering process, which I'll discuss in the next chapter. Mastering is not something I would recommend amateur or novice recorders to try to do alone. If you're forced to master your finished product to get it to broadcast quality, there is computer software available to assist you. I recommend consulting an engineer on the best product for your platform and the format for which you hope to master, and proceed from there. There are plenty mastering software products

FIGURE 7.7 Mastering engineer at work behind a control board. Photo courtesy of Airshow Mastering, Takoma Park, MD; Randy Leroy, engineer.

available for download free of charge. Just remember the old adage about getting what you pay for. In all cases, make sure you have a backup copy of your recording available in case your computer crashes, or somehow you lose your final mix. Technology giveth, and sometimes technology taketh away. Figure 7.7 shows a mastering engineer mastering a recording.

Summary

Using a mixing board is an electronic way for you to fine-tune your group's performance. Familiarizing yourself with a mixer or soundboard will help you to manipulate recorded sound the same way you manipulate live sound. Mixing boards should not be adjusted during the actual performance. If you want to shape the sound of your group, you should set the board during your sound check. Always try to have a backup copy of your recording in case something happens during the mixing process. You don't need to have a complete understanding of a mixing board to achieve what you want to do to mix your recording. You will need to understand how to use gain to import sound, faders to export sounds (volumes), and EQ knobs to adjust highs, mids, and lows to shape the sound characteristics of instruments and voices. A lot of EQ adjustments can be achieved by turning the knobs on a particular channel until the sound feels right to you. You can experiment and tweak the sound until you're ready to export it for the final mix. Digital mixers allow you to achieve this with preprogrammed adjustments. Because digital recorders are able to do it to multiple tracks at the same time, they are cost- and time-efficient.

8

Mastering a Performance

Chapter 7 discussed what a mixer is and how it is used during the recording process. This chapter will discuss using a mixer or digital workstation to master a performance and the wisdom of outsourcing your mastering. Of all the things done in the recording process, mastering is the most important. If mixing is cutting the diamond from the diamond in the rough, mastering is polishing the diamond and preparing it for purchase. Throughout the book I've been talking about the best ways to do your own recording, so it may seem inconsistent that when discussing mastering, I'm encouraging you to outsource the work. I'm suggesting this because your project is so important that you don't want poor mastering to negate all of your hard work. There are numerous mastering software products available to use; if you can take the time to learn how to use them, they will suffice under most circumstances. So what is mastering, and why do you need to understand the mastering process?

What is mastering?

Mastering is preparing your recording for broadcast quality on all available formats. That means live streaming, CDs, MP3 or MP4, and all other current and future formats. The idea is to get the best finished product possible. If you have recorded different songs or groups and want to compile them on a single broadcast format, mastering enables you to do the following: have a consistent quality of sound; have balance in the recordings (keeping one song or group from being louder or softer than another); have space that feels natural between songs; have consistent highs and lows (equalization or EQ); and having a clean, polished sound. The technical definition of mastering is the process of transferring a recorded audio final mix to a storage device (i.e., the master). This master is the source from which all copies will be produced. Figure 8.1 shows a mastering control room board.

FIGURE 8.1 A mastering control room board. Photo courtesy of Airshow Mastering, Takoma Park, MD.

Getting a good master

Getting a good master means starting with a good final mix. This final mix must contain the finished product, from which all copies will be produced from the master at the highest broadcast level. That means that all balances and any cleaning up of the recording must be finished by the time you go to mastering. Most engineers will proof your final mix in mono to determine what tweaking needs to be done before and during mastering. Because mastering generally requires going to a studio and working with a trained engineer, it's not my intention to attempt to train you to prepare a master; my intent is to make you aware of this final step. A master will be prepared whether you've used two microphones or multiple microphones. Mass production or duplication cannot be done from the final mix unless it has been mastered. Figure 8.2 shows the layout of a mastering studio.

What are the final steps?

Just as microphones are the most important part of recording, monitors and headphones are the most important parts of mastering. You have to be able to hear what you have on the final mix in order to start the final steps of mastering. The final steps are to prepare

FIGURE 8.2 An interior view of a mastering studio. Photo courtesy of Airshow Mastering, Takoma Park, MD.

your final mix for mastering and to make sure the master can be used for whatever format you plan to use for your finished product. The most important part of this process is selecting a good mastering facility. Since mastering can be done without your being present, you can send your final mix to any mastering facility. This means that you don't have to have a mastering studio near you. Technology exists that allows you to submit your recording to a mastering studio through fiber optic phone lines without having a physical copy. Figure 8.3 shows mastering equipment using fiber optics to receive a master received from an outside source.

Some mastering facilities will even allow you to attach WAV files or MP3s to emails. All you need is a system that can transmit large files via email (Dropbox, FileMaker, and others). If you plan to produce a CD, CD manufacturers will do the mastering for you. Since you won't be there for the mastering, it's important that you provide complete instructions and directions for the mastering engineer. You don't want to take for granted that the engineer has or has had experience mastering school projects. Equalizing and volume adjustments sometimes have to be made during the mastering process. Make sure your manufacturer sends you a proof for your approval before mass production begins. You've worked too hard for a problem to occur at this step. Most CD manufacturers provide you with a form that allows you to give them final instructions. If you've done mastering before you go to manufacturing, you have to send the facility a master and safety backup master for them to make the glass master, which they will use

FIGURE 8.3 Mastering equipment using fiber optics to receive a master received from an outside source. Photo courtesy of Mike Monseur, Bias Mastering Studio, Springfield, VA.

to make mass copies of your CD. Figure 8.4 shows the computer program screen used while creating a glass master.

Nonmusical things such as artwork, liner notes (a written description of the project), acknowledgments, and personnel, song, and composer names will all need to be included with the master. You will also need to go to Songfile.com (the Harry Fox agency), ASCAP, BMI, or individual song publishers for permission to release the recording for sale or broadcast.

Mastering yourself

Even though I advise against undertaking the mastering process yourself, should you decide to do it, here are things you must consider. If you did the final mix, you're in a very good position to do the mastering. The best masters are done because care was taken with the final mix. Something seemingly as small as too much bass or upper parts shrinks the ceiling of the recording. That means that the volume levels for the master are limited by the unbalanced sound mixed in. This is why engineers listen in mono for proofing the final mix. Any sounds that dominate the mono playback alert you to the problems you'll face in mastering. You can use EQ in mastering to adjust the highs and lows, but

FIGURE 8.4 Shows the computer program screen used while creating a glass master. Photo courtesy of Mike Monseur, Bias Mastering Studio, Springfield, VA.

any balance problems within the mix can't be reset during mastering; you must go back and adjust the mix. Think of it like this: mastering is polishing the mix as a whole, while mixing is adjusting all of the parts for a good balance. To use a food analogy, if you use too much salt in your recipe, you can't take it out of the finished product; salt will dominate the overall taste. In music, too much trumpet in the mix will mean that the trumpet sound will dominate the master. Test your mix in mono by turning off the stereo panning on your master bus. This helps you hear whether any instrument's volume is out of balance with others. If you hear any unbalanced sound during the mono playback, go back into the mix and make corrections before proceeding to mastering. Even though you're equalizing the entire song, make sure that you spend the time getting each instrument equalized as best as you can in the mix. There's no shortcut here. You must listen carefully to the playback of the final mix knowing that what you hear will be exactly what your mastered copy will sound like. Remember, the volume you're controlling during the mix is the volume of the overall track, not individual parts of that track.

Finalizing your master

The finished product of your master should sound exactly like what you'd expect to hear on a radio broadcast or a live stream. The space between songs should feel comfortable. If you have a song in multiple movements, the space between movements should sound exactly as it would if you were conducting live (especially if you recorded movements separately). Space between songs should have a comfortable amount of time between them. There is no set amount of seconds between songs; as you listen you will hear what seems comfortable to the listener. During mastering you can add "hall effects." This means that you can adjust the reverb to imitate the sound of different-sized halls. It's best to choose one that simulates the performance space where the recording took place.

Remember, if you're doing your own mastering, the idea is to get as close to the results you'd get from a studio master. Take time out to listen to your final mix on different speakers, and take good notes on what you hear. A trained engineer can hear things in a recording you may not hear as easily. Does it sound too quiet? Is it muddy, or does it have poor balances such as too much bass (or too much cowbell)? Mastering is not easy for engineers, so don't expect it to be easy for you. Get a musician whose ear you trust to listen to your final mix on her speakers and compare her opinions with your notes.

There's software like Sony Soundforge, Ableton, Logic, or free downloads like Audacity that can help you. Each of the mastering software packages requires you to import your final mix, so remember to have a backup copy before starting. There are also many tutorials on YouTube and elsewhere on the Internet that can walk you through the process. Once again, if you can go to a professional facility for mastering, go. You'll need to have a good set of speakers and a good set of audio headphones in order to proof your mix and master. You don't want problems with sound reproduction to cause you to think that there are problems with your mix or master. Low-end speakers may give you too much or too little bass. If you make adjustments and then listen to the master on better monitors, you may discover that you need more or less bass in your master. The mistake most often made by nonstudio mastering is that the volume is too quiet. Most engineers try to get the loudest signal with the most dynamic contrast possible. Earlier in the book I described how one of my best recordings was ruined because the person recording it adjusted our lower dynamics up and our louder dynamics down, leaving a flat recording with no contrast. This often happens with home mastering.

Distortion (too much signal) and dropouts (too little signal) are the most common mistakes amateur mastering engineers make. Your mastering software will have limiters and compressors that allow you to load in a basic preset that will help you where your untrained engineering ear may fail you. A limiter or compressor will reduce in volume any sounds that exceed the set volume threshold. Trained engineers know this based on their knowledge of high decibel levels. Your software will do it for you as long as you set the loudest levels in the preset (most digital mixers do this also). As you can see, much goes into the mastering process. If you've gone through the processes described in this book to get a good recording, don't ruin everything by doing a poor job mastering. Diamond cutters who destroy diamonds don't last too long, and neither do poor mastering engineers!

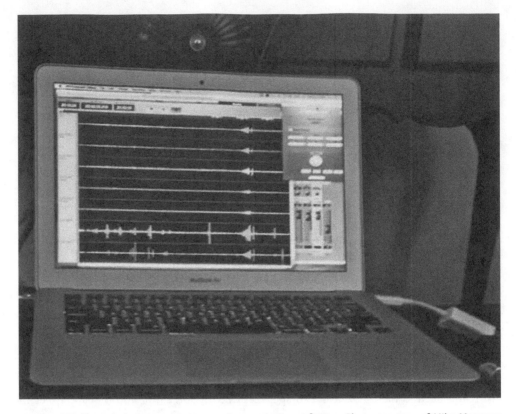

FIGURE 8.5 Shows a laptop computer running mastering software. Photo courtesy of Mike Monseur, Bias Mastering Studio, Springfield, VA.

Summary

A good master is the result of a good mix. Take care in proofing your mix to make sure there is no sound that sticks out. If possible, get a professional audio mastering engineer to complete this step. Prepare your master for all available broadcast formats. Make sure that if you have to export your mix, you have a safety or backup copy. If you're not comfortable mastering yourself, don't do it. If you're not familiar with the basics of EQ, don't attempt to master your recording yourself. I've used the diamond cutter analogy often, but imagine finding a priceless diamond in the rough and deciding to cut it and polish it yourself after reading books on cutting diamonds. If you budget correctly at the beginning of your project, you'll have enough money to cover mastering costs. Mastering is not the place in your budget to skimp. Figure 8.5 shows a laptop computer running mastering software.

9

Developing a Budget

Purchasing the correct equipment for your recording is the most important first step. You should make sure that whatever funds you need can be obtained from your school or your school district. Some schools will allow you to purchase equipment through your library or media program, technology funds, or audiovisual (A/V) funds. If these funds are available you should use them, because there will be less required from your budget. In case you have to use your own funds, wise purchases will be needed. The amount of money you allot to purchase microphones or a soundboard may impact funds you will need for other purposes. Since this is a departmental expense, the costs should be shared by all groups who plan to use the equipment (bands, orchestras, choral groups, guitar ensembles, etc.). This may also include the drama department if the microphones will be used for musicals or other drama productions. There is also the possibility of including this equipment in the auditorium's A/V budget. Explore all possibilities for funding before exhausting your band, orchestra, or chorus budget. Usually, school districts provide funds for new equipment or equipment replacement purchases every two to five years. Just as planning the recording is important, researching the purchasing of equipment is important. School districts have bid lists that will include vendors who carry the equipment you'll need. If your school is up for capital improvements, a studio-quality soundboard is not out of the question for your auditorium. These large boards can cost anywhere from $1,999.00 to $20,000.00 and are permanently built into the auditorium's control room. Figure 9.1 is a lower cost permanent control room console.

How much should be spent on equipment?

In order to determine how much your budget should be, you will need to make an itemized list of equipment needed. While determining the equipment that's needed, you

FIGURE 9.1 A lower cost permanent large control room console. Photo courtesy of Behringer.

should consider exactly what you will need the equipment for. To do that, you must consider the size of your group and the venues in which you plan to record. Recording in a large room may require you to have more microphones, a soundboard, and funds to go to a studio for postproduction. If you decide you're going to need a soundboard, that will probably be the most expensive item that you'll need to purchase (from $599.00 to $1,999.00, depending on the number of channels). The next high cost will be the amount for postproduction. Postproduction will involve taking or sending your recording to a professional recording or mastering facility where you'll have to pay studio hourly or project rates ($125.00 per hour or higher). Depending on the soundboard you choose, you may be able to do your own mixing. This returns us to the ongoing theme of this book: planning in advance.

The cost of microphones will be determined by the following: polar patterns (pickup patterns) that will be needed, the number of microphones, the type and brand of microphone, the number of stands needed, microphone cables, and any accessories needed for the microphones. Most audio suppliers bundle microphones with all of the accessories needed, so shop wisely for savings. As discussed in previous chapters, microphones are the center point for gathering the best sounds. In essence, they are your electronic ears.

Where can I get the funding for equipment?

There are many sources for funding that may be available to you: the school, your parents' group, your school district, and, in some cases, from your state. Let's look at each of these one by one. First, in your school there are a few possibilities: departmental funds, cooperative funding between departments, and school-wide funds provided by your administration. If your department receives an allocation of funds annually for equipment, some of those funds can be used to purchase equipment that will be shared. This means that if you're recording a joint concert or separate concerts, you're going to use some of the same microphones. If this is the case, microphones purchased should be good for recording voices and instruments. Usually, those microphones are more expensive because voices don't produce the volume and intensity of instruments. The microphones will need to be sensitive enough to record voices but not so sensitive that too much intensity destroys the microphone or distorts the sound (some ribbon microphones are not good for recording instruments). With about a thousand dollars of combined funds you should be able to get microphones that suit your needs plus cables and stands for the department. In Appendix A I have listed microphone brands, types, and general suggested retail costs from the manufacturer to help you select microphones that may suit your budget. This is why a working knowledge of condenser microphones and dynamic microphones is needed (see chapters 1 and 2).

If the music department and the drama program in your school have a need for microphones for musicals, you may be able to use what's called cooperative or interdepartmental funds for purchases (the terms vary from school to school). Besides funds raised from performances, most high schools allocate funds for drama productions, especially musicals. Microphones fall under production costs. Musicals generally require the use of wireless clip-on or head-worn microphones. Figure 9.2 shows a wireless head-worn system.

These microphones can be used by show choirs or any other choral groups that move. Of course, should you purchase microphones with these funds, be sure to have a calendar of use to make certain that there are no conflicts between users. You may want to record something away from school while the drama department is using the equipment in school. These funds, however, are a good source for the purchase of high-cost items such as a stationary soundboard. These soundboards are built into a control room in the auditorium, so they will be linked to microphone inputs on the stage and walls in the auditorium (this is why they may fall under capital improvement funds). This means that school equipment funds can possibly be used. Every year the administration is allocated funds from the district for new equipment, replacements, and upgrades. Do your research, and find out what percentage of these funds you can tap into.

Your parents' organization is also there to assist you with fundraising. At the beginning of the year you should be prepared to give them a detailed budget. Microphones or a soundboard should be a one-time expense. The parents' group may have fundraising options that are not available to you.

The National Association for Music Education (NAfME) provides music educators with guidelines for parent-booster groups and how to manage fundraising. Check their website for guidance (www.nafme.org).

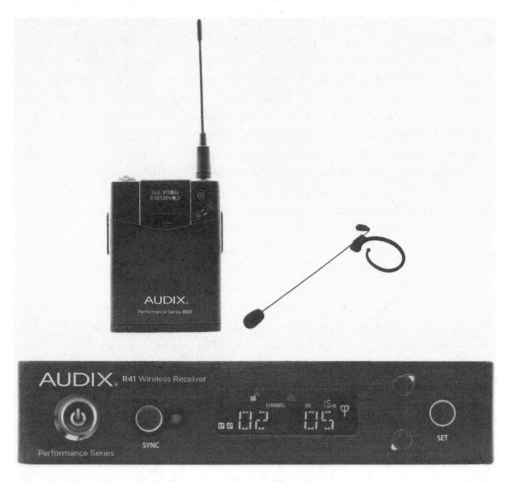

FIGURE 9.2 A head-worn wireless microphone system for vocalists. Photo used by permission of Audix Corporation, Wilsonville, OR.

How much can I expect to spend on equipment?

Microphones range in cost from less than a hundred dollars to over three thousand dollars. The cost of a microphone or microphone pair will depend on the kind of microphone (condenser or dynamic) and the quality of manufacturing. Brands made in the United States are generally found on school bid lists and are good quality. Brands made in Germany are found at the high end of cost and quality. There are other European and Japanese brands that fall in between the cost of American-made and German-made. The amount you spend will depend on usage and durability. Studios can afford to spend thousands on one microphone because professionals will be handling them, but since most schools don't have professional sound engineers on staff, it's not practical to purchase microphones that can't be replaced because of the cost. Determining how much you have to spend, you should take into consideration how much it would cost to replace damaged or stolen equipment as well as the initial purchase. There are very good microphones that can be purchased from $150 to $200 apiece. Most stereo pairs are sold together to make sure you have a matched pair for best recording results.

If possible, solicit the help of an audio professional for recommendations and poll other educators to find out which brands work for them. There are many music educator forums on the Internet that can help you. Shure Microphones maintains a blog that discusses the use of their microphones in educational settings, and other manufacturers like Neumann, AKG, and Sennheiser maintain help lines and blogs. Because they are aware of school budget limitations they will talk you through the planning, purchasing, and use of their microphones, as well as which ones will best suit your purposes. We're back to the recurring theme: planning. Because microphones can be expensive to purchase and replace, you'll need to have a secure storage area. Microphones can easily fit into backpacks and pockets, so security is necessary. They should be stored in areas that have low-volume traffic. You don't want microphones to be dropped or knocked over even if they're in a protective case.

If you decide to order microphones from the Internet, order from a company like Sweetwater or directly from the manufacturer. You don't want to order a used microphone or a microphone from a third party because the ribbon, coil, or diaphragm may be damaged. You may seem to be saving money, but you risk ending up with unexpected expenses from replacing useless equipment. Some recording studios may have used microphones for sale, but arrange for a trial period if possible. Ordering on consignment may be possible if ordering used or second-hand equipment.

When possible, order microphones in pairs. For most of the configurations described in the book, a matched pair of microphones will be needed. If you know you're going to be using M/S recording, you won't need a matched pair. A pair of cardioid or supercardioid microphones gives you the greatest flexibility should you decide on a matched pair.

Hand-held devices

If your budget cannot afford pairs of microphones, hand-held digital recorders are your best alternative. These devices can yield good recordings. Figure 9.3 shows Zoom handheld devices.

Depending on the group and the recording space, hand-held devices can get broadcast quality recordings. Most of these devices cost less than three hundred dollars. If you need time to raise funds for microphones and soundboards, hand-held devices will be sufficient substitutes. Be aware that hand-held devices aren't going to yield the same quality recordings as a good condenser pair, but they will give you a suitable recording for mixing. The biggest drawbacks of these devices is the loss of high-pitched instruments, clipping, and distortion. Some of the more expensive units even record high-pitched instruments well, but cost the same as a pair of condenser microphones. If you're

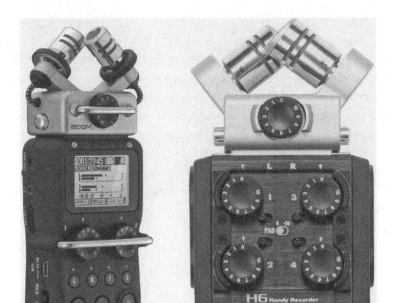

FIGURE 9.3 A pair of Zoom hand-held devices. Photos used by permission of Zoom, North America.

going to record inside an auditorium, a stereo pair is best. If you're going to record outside often, hand-held devices are your best and most practical choice. You can choose to use a hand-held device or a microphone attachment for a phone or tablet. Figure 9.4 shows hand-held device attachments used with cell phones.

Soundboards

Buying a soundboard should be a one-time purchase. In previous chapters I've mentioned that a ten channel soundboard should suffice. Depending on whether you purchase a stand-alone soundboard or a digital workstation, the cost can be held between $1,500.00 to $2,500.00. Of course, you may opt to purchase a six-or-eight channel board depending on your needs. Remember, since it's probably going to be a one-time purchase, plan for your needs five years in the future. Don't skimp on a smaller board and later discover that your program outgrows what you have. It is better to have more channels than you need than not enough. Unused channels won't affect your recording. As with microphone purchases, avoid buying used equipment unless you can test the board and verify that all patches, inputs, and outputs work. Your microphones are only as good as your soundboard allows them to be.

When developing your budget, write out an itemized list of costs. Use the information in the earlier chapters to decide on exactly what you need, and then do some comparative shopping. Most vendors will have beginning-of-the-year or year-end sales. I have found year-end sales best for purchasing higher-priced items because vendors are trying to clear inventory to make room for newer models or to sell overstocked items. If you're fortunate enough to make purchases for a new school, you may be able to get volume deals if the vendor is supplying other equipment to your school or school district. Your district's bid list may have special discounts factored in. Ask questions and solicit assistance. If your school has a business manager, he may have a relationship with vendors who supply audiovisual equipment. Don't be afraid to ask for help.

FIGURE 9.4 Shows a Zoom microphone attachment for an iPhone or tablet. Photos used by permission of Zoom, North America.

Sample budget

As a simple guide for a moderate-costs budget, here is a sample of what should be included. Prices are from Sweetwater.com. If you want to use X/Y or parallel pairs with matching microphones, you can expect to pay around $99.00 each for two Shure SM58 or SM57 microphones. These are dynamic microphones. If you want Shure MX150 cardioid condenser microphones, they cost around $199.00 each. Microphone stands cost from $29.00 to $199.00 each. Mogami microphone cables (discussed in detail in the next chapter) run approximately $49.95 for ten-foot or $54.95 for fifteen-foot, each with gold contacts. Cables can cost as little as $9.99, but remember that cables affect the amount of noise that seeps into recordings no matter how good the microphones or soundboards are. A cheap cable can ruin a recording. Should you need a soundboard or mixer, you

FIGURE 9.5 Shows an analog mixer and a digital mixer with travel case. Photo courtesy of Behringer.

can get a Behringer Europower PMP 1680S ten-channel mixer for around $449.00 or a Mackie 1642VLZ4 Analog mixer for approximately $699.00. Shure has a four-channel microphone mixer that can be used as an affordable starter kit that currently sells for $279.00. Remember, this should be a last resort if you expect your program to grow. If you don't plan to do a lot of mixing that requires the use of effects, this model is practical. So based on these prices, you can have a budget of $1,500.00 and get everything you need. Appendix A has a list of recommended microphones and Appendix B has a list of soundboards and mixers. The models recommended are based on recommendations from audio engineers and music teachers who have used them. There are many good models that can be found at Sweetwater and other vendors. Figure 9.5 shows an affordable analog and an affordable digital mixer with travel case.

Summary

Be sure to develop an itemized list of equipment needed. Once you formulate your list, check the cost of equipment in order to get the most for your money spent. Develop your budget and find ways to gain funds or funding. As you develop your budget, plan for five-year growth, not just for your current needs. Seek out individuals who can advise you. Ask questions and get advice from sales consultants, manufacturers, music educators, and audio professionals.

10

Selecting the Best Equipment

Selecting the best equipment is an important step as you plan your recording project. Price is not always the best indicator as to whether you are getting the right equipment for your needs. There are numerous moderately priced microphones and mixing boards that will suit your purposes of recording and mixing a good live rehearsal or performance. Many of the things that have been discussed in previous chapters will help determine what microphones are best for you. The room size, microphone setup, microphone polarity, proximity, and the number of microphones that will be used all affect the kind that are needed. The most important thing to consider when choosing a microphone is how you plan to use it: will you be using it onstage for instrumental groups, vocal groups, or to microphone an instrument or vocal soloist? Getting duplicates of the same microphone may not be the best way for you to achieve a good recording, but most recording techniques require matching pairs of microphones.

What should be considered when deciding on microphones?

The most important thing that should be considered when deciding on microphones is the size of the area in which the microphones will be used. Most cardioid microphones work well in small or large spaces. Supercardioid microphones are good for focusing on specific sections, voices or instruments. Omni microphones are good for recording general areas, and when used as a parallel pair will collect the most sound from your sound source (all condenser microphones make good parallel pairs). In order to know which microphone is best, you must consider the room size and the probable output of your sound source. A band or large orchestra can be recorded quite well with a pair of omni microphones. A pair of cardioid microphones as a parallel pair or in X/Y or M/S configuration will also suffice in most cases. Figure 10.1 is a picture of X/Y pairs.

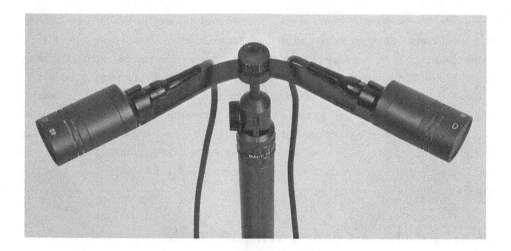

FIGURE 10.1 A matching pair of microphones in X/Y Blumlein setup. Used by permission of Neumann, Berlin.

Because the polarity of cardioid microphones will record a wide heart-shaped area and very little or nothing from behind, they are sometimes a better choice than an omni microphone, which records from all directions. Lower-quality microphones will have more dropouts or losses of signal than higher-quality microphones (dynamic microphones versus condenser microphones). This doesn't mean you should spend money on high-end condenser microphones that may need additional equipment such as preamps to power them. This also doesn't mean you have to buy low-end ribbon microphones. Ribbon microphones are generally poor choices to record an entire sound source, but they may be adequate to record specific instruments or specific sections. Some engineers prefer ribbon microphones for figure-of-eight recording (used for M/S). The biggest reason to avoid using ribbon microphones on loud sound sources is that the ribbon may be overloaded and become damaged. Ribbon microphones should not be used to record snare drums or jazz band drum sets; the ribbon will be damaged. Once the ribbon is damaged, there will be no more undistorted sound recorded. If you have chosen to use a ribbon microphone, you may not discover that you've lost the recording until after the performance. Ribbon microphones do well in figure-of-eight recording because they are a distance away from the sound source. Ribbon microphones can also be damaged by phantom power or poor quality cables. Condenser microphones have additional power that helps them avoid the problems ribbon microphones may have. Your budgetary constraints may cause you to choose ribbon microphones. If so, know that you can get a good recording through good microphone placement and proximity. Ask the sales consultant about this before purchasing.

What kinds of cables will be best?

Generally, when you purchase microphones, all of the cables you need come with the microphones. High-end cables can come with gold tips or expensive metals. Some cables come with better internal wires than others. The point of using good cables is to avoid signal loss between the microphone and the soundboard. Good cables should not be placed across electric cables, because they'll pick up the hum of electrical current going

FIGURE 10.2 Mogami gold-tip cables. Used by permission of Marshall Electronics.

through the wires. This happens with better cables but is sometimes confused with being a sign of a low-quality cable. Most high-quality cables use copper for good conductivity, and if you wish to know which cables are best for you and whether your microphones need low impedance or high-impedance cables, go to the microphone manufacturer's web site. Mogami cables are the gold standard of microphone cables and are described by most professional engineers as producing the purest sound of any cable on the market. Figure 10.2 shows Mogami gold tip cables.

What kind of mixing board is needed?

The audio mixer or soundboard combines audio signals, processes the signals, and then routes them. A mixing board is one of the keys to collecting sound for a good recording. One of the first concerns is to choose a mixer or soundboard that has enough inputs for your use. If you're using multiple microphones, you'll need a mixer with multiple inputs. A ten-channel analog mixer (a mixer with ten inputs) is the most practical for school groups because it takes up to ten microphones and is portable enough to take along for remote (nonstudio) recordings. There are six- and eight-channel soundboards, but a ten-channel board is the wisest choice economically. Some affordable sixteen-track soundboards have ten inputs and cost the same as eight- or ten-channel boards. There are lots of good choices for school budgets to handle. Sometimes you'll see "live sound mixers" and "studio mixers." For your purposes there's a thin line between choosing one over the other. You'll be recording live sound in an attempt to get a studio-quality recording. Because of this, ask the sales consultant questions based on how you plan to use the equipment and where you plan to use it. In some cases, studio mixers refers to mixers that are not designed to be transported. This is a major distinction, because it may mean that you can only set it up in one location. A list of brands and suggested retail prices can be found in Appendix B.

In order to choose and purchase a mixing board, there are a few terms with which you must be familiar. Previously I've stated that a ten-channel mixer should be sufficient for your needs.

A channel is a signal path. A mixer with a large channel count allows more things to be connected. Channels are usually designed to take microphones and some other devices such as amplifiers, preamps, or signal processors. If you're recording a jazz ensemble or jazz or show choir or any group using electronics, amplifiers can be run through the board to achieve a balanced live sound and capture enough sound for the recording (digital mixers are best for external devices). A channel strip is a group of circuits and controls that function together on an individual mixer channel to affect the audio signals that pass through it. The strip allows you to design the sound by tweaking the highs, mids, and lows of the inputted sound. You can also add EQ and reverb on one channel without affecting any other channel. Each channel has a place in the back or front for connections (XLR, quarter-inch TRS, or RCA inputs). XLR inputs are balanced

FIGURE 10.3 Shows the cable inputs on the front and back of mixers. Photo courtesy of Behringer.

to minimize interference and noise. Other inputs accept RCA or quarter-inch tip-ring-sleeve (TRS) connectors. Figure 10.3 shows the inputs for XLR and RCA type connectors.

If you're recording jazz groups or jazz choirs, you'll need enough inputs and outputs (I/O) to connect microphones, amps, instruments, and monitors. Monitors are speakers used on stage facing the sound source so that performers can hear themselves. If monitors are used during the recording, there will be a need to have someone working the soundboard for live sound. The live or house sound won't necessarily affect the recording, depending on the buses used to feed the recording device, but having someone monitor the input is always wise. Remember that adjustments should not be made during the performance. This refers to the recording input and output. The house sound will need to be monitored during the performance. Once the gains and output have been set for the recording, it's as if there are two boards in use. Figure 10.4 shows the recording output slides on the far right.

FIGURE 10.4 Shows the output sliders and knobs on an analog mixing board. Photo courtesy of Behringer.

Preamps

A microphone preamplifier is a sound device that prepares a microphone signal to be processed by other equipment. Because microphone signals are often too weak to be transmitted to mixing consoles and recording devices with adequate quality, a preamp is needed. Preamplifiers increase a microphone signal to line-level (the level of signal strength required by such devices) by providing stable gain (input coming in) while preventing induced noise that would otherwise distort the signal. Figure 10.5 shows an external preamplifier unit.

If needed, your choice of a microphone preamplifier will play a significant role in the final sound of your recording. Some microphone preamps have more than one output, so it's not uncommon to see an XLR output and a 1/4″ TRS output on the same preamp to give you more connection options. Preamps with multiple outputs will allow you to run multiple microphones through the preamp. This is only necessary if you're using multiple condenser microphones. Some condenser microphones have internal preamps that function in the same way as the external unit. Figure 10.6 shows a small preamp attachment.

Some microphone preamps have a built-in analog and digital (A/D) converter, which allows you to run a digital signal out of the preamp directly to your recording

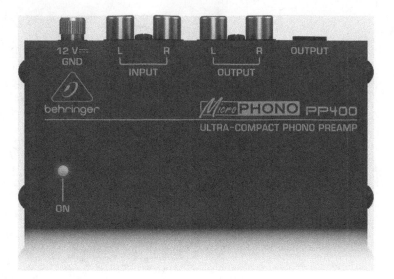

FIGURE 10.5 Shows an external preamp unit. Photo courtesy of Behringer.

FIGURE 10.6 Shows a preamp attachment for a microphone. Copyright Shure Incorporated; used with permission.

device. This means you will typically achieve a lower "noise floor" than you would with an analog connection. The noise floor is defined as the measure of the signal created from the sum of all sources and unwanted signals within a measurement system. This is something best discussed with an audio sales consultant so that you don't purchase something that you don't need or won't be able to master for best use. Use the technical information provided here so that you to have the best information to use to question the sales consultant.

Since the soundboard or mixer will record your sound and then will also be the place where you will mix the finished recording, it's important that you get the best value for your money spent. This is another case in which no matter how good your microphones are, an inadequate soundboard can ruin the recording. If you're not purchasing the microphones and soundboard from the same vendor, describe your equipment so that you can get a good match. There are some microphones that work better with some soundboard circuitry than others. Ask an audio consultant which brands match best. Obviously, if the microphones and soundboards are manufactured by the same company, compatibility is not an issue.

Summary

When choosing equipment, don't be confused by price. If you ask the right questions and adequately describe your needs, you can get the best equipment for a good price. Avoid the tendency to overbuy. Don't purchase equipment that will sit on a shelf because you never use it. Measure your rehearsal area and get size specs of your auditorium so that you know what range your microphones need to have. Decide which polar patterns will best suit your needs. If you purchase microphones that depend on preamplifiers, be sure to match them during the purchase. There is no need to buy a preamp for

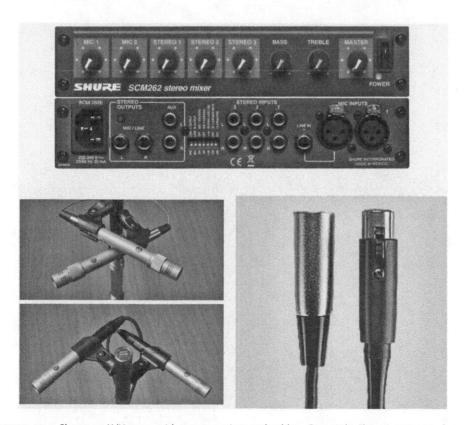

FIGURE 10.7 Shows an X/Y setup with a stereo mixer and cables. Copyright Shure Incorporated; used with permission.

microphones with built-in preamplifiers. Once again, planning and asking questions will save you money and help you make wise purchases. Purchase your equipment with at least a five-year life span. This is where price may be an indication of quality; choose wisely. Figure 10.7 shows the minimum amount of equipment needed if you can't buy a ten-channel soundboard.

Microphones

Here are the suggested retail prices for microphones described in the book.

CARDIOID CONDENSER MICROPHONES

Shure MX150	$199.00
Shure Beta 181/C	$499.00
Sennheiser ME 4	$149.95
Telefunken M60	$595.00
AKG C 214	$399.99
AKG C 391 B	$499.99
AKG C 5 (Vocal)	$179.00
Shure GLX-D Digital Wireless System	$549.00
Shure GLX-D Digital Wireless System	$519.00
Neumann KM 184	$849.00
Neumann TLM 49	$1,699.95
Neumann TLM 193	$1,599.95
Neumann BCM 104	$1,079.95
Neumann KMS 104	$699.95
Rode M5 Matched pair	$199.00
Rode NT1-A Single	$229.00
Rode NT5 - Matched pair	$429.00
Rode NTK Large-diaphragm	$529.00
Rode NT4 Cardioid Condenser XY Stereo	$529.00

SUPER CARDIOID MICROPHONES

Shure Super 55 Deluxe	$249.00
AKG P5 Supercardioid (Vocal)	$89.00
Sennheiser MME 865-1 BK – 865	$299.95

HEADWORN MICROPHONES

AKG C 555 L	$139.99
AKG C 520	$219.00
AKG C 520 L	$179.00
Sennheiser ME 3	$159.95
Countryman E6 Omnidirectional Earset for Shure	$389.00
Countryman E6 for Sennheiser	$399.00
Audio-Technica BP894	$449.00
Audio-Technica BP894cW-TH	$349.00
Line 6 HS30 - Headset Mic	$69.00

DYNAMIC MICROPHONES

Shure SM58	$99.00
Shure SM57	$99.00
Shure Beta 58A	$159.00
Samson Q1U	$49.99
Behringer XM1800S	$39.99
AKG P120	$99.00
AKG P170	$99.00

Mixing and Soundboards

Here are the suggested retail prices for the mixing/soundboards described in the book.

Allen & Heath Qu-16 Chrome Edition Digital Mixer with 16 Channels	$1,999.00
Allen & Heath Qu-24 Chrome Edition 24-channel Digital Console	$2,499.99
Allen & Heath Qu-32 Chrome Edition 32-channel Digital Console	$2,999.99
Allen & Heath WZ4:16:2 16-channel Stereo Mixer	$999.00
Allen & Heath ZED-12FX 12-channel Mixer	$499.00
Allen & Heath ZED-22 FX 22-channel Mixer	$799.00
Behringer Europower PMP1680S 10-channel, 1600W Powered Mixer	$449.99
Behringer Europower PMP4000 16-channel, 1600W Powered Mixer	$499.99
Behringer Europower PMP6000 20-channel, 1,600W Powered Mixer	$599.99
Behringer X32 Compact 40-input, 25-total-bus Digital Mixer	$1,799.99
Behringer X32 Compact-TP 40-input, 25-total-bus Digital Mixer	$1,999.99
Behringer X32 Producer 40-input, 25-total-bus Digital Mixer	$1,499.99
Behringer X32-TP 40-input, 25-total-bus Digital Mixer	$2,699.99
Mackie ProFX12v2 12-ch Analog Mixer	$249.00
Mackie 1604VLZ4 16-ch Analog Mixer	$899.99
Mackie 1642VLZ4 16-ch Analog Mixer	$699.99
Mackie 2404VLZ4 24-ch Analog Mixer with 20 Onyx Mic Preamps	$1,149.99
Mackie ProFX12v2 12-channel Compact Mixer with Built-in Effects and USB	$279.99
Mackie ProFX16v2 16-channel, 4-bus Mixer	$499.99
Mackie ProFX22v2 22-channel, 4-bus Mixer	$649.99
Midas M32R 40-channel Digital Mixing Console	$2,999.00
Midas VeniceF24–24 Channel Firewire 24-channel 4-bus Analog Mixer	$1,859.00

Midas VeniceF32–32 Channel Firewire 32-channel 4-bus Analog Mixer	$2,219.00
Peavey PV 20 USB 20-channel Mixer with 16 Mic Preamps	$549.99
Peavey XR 1212 Powered Mixer12-channel	$1,099.99
PreSonus StudioLive 16.0.2 16-channel Digital Mixer	$999.00
PreSonus StudioLive 16.4.2AI 16-channel Digital Mixer	$1,599.95
PreSonus StudioLive 24.4.2AI 24-channel Digital Mixer	$1,899.95
PreSonus StudioLive 32.4.2AI 32-channel Digital Mixer	$2299.95
Roland AIRA MX-1 Mix Performer 18-channel Performance Mixer	$599.00
Soundcraft Signature 12 MTK 12-channel Mixer	$449.00
Soundcraft Signature 16 16-ch Mixer	$599.00
Soundcraft Signature 22 MTK 22-channel Mixer	$799.00
Yamaha EMX5016CF 16-input, 1000W Powered Mixer	$999.99
Yamaha EMX512SC Powered Mixer with 500W per Channel	$569.99
Yamaha MG20XU 20-channel Analog Mixer with 16 Microphone Preamps	$699.95
Yamaha TF1–16 Channel 16-channel, 40-input Digital Mixer	$2,499.99
Yamaha TF5–32 Channel 32-channel, 48-input Digital Mixer	$3,599.99

Glossary

Ambience—the character and atmosphere of a place

Ambient sounds—background noise added to a recording to give the impression that it was recorded live

Axis—a fixed reference point for the recording of sound

Blocking—the physical arrangement of actors or singers on a stage

Buses—circuit intersections where the output from several channels meet

Cardioid—a directional microphone with a pattern of a heart-shaped curve

Channel—a signal path on a soundboard or mixer

Channel strip—a group of circuits and controls that function together on a mixer channel to affect the audio signals that pass through it

Digital audio interface—converts binary information into audio information

Digital audio workstation—a device for recording, editing, and producing audio files

Decca tree—the use of a three-microphone setup using three directional microphones to record sounds from the left, center, and right sides of a sound source

Figure-of-eight—a recording technique having the polar pattern the shape of an eight

Hypercardioid—microphones with a very narrow heart-shaped polar pattern

Impedance—the effective resistance of an electric circuit or component to alternating current

Master—a storage device from which all duplicates of a recording are made

Mastering—the process of transferring a recorded audio final mix to a storage device

Microphone—an instrument used for converting sound waves into electrical energy variations

Mid-side—use of a mid microphone and directional microphone to create a realistic stereo image

Mix—a process for merging recorded tracks into a single output

Mixer—a device for merging input signals to produce a combined output in the form of sound

Noise floor—the measure of the signal created by the sum of all noise sources

Omnidirectional—receiving signals from or transmitting in all directions

Patch—a panel that contains rows of input and output jacks

Phase—the relationship and time between the successive states or cycles of an oscillating or repeating system; a time shift

Phase cancellation—when two signals of the same frequency are put out of phase with each other

Playback—the reproduction of previously recorded sounds

Polar patterns—the pickup patterns of a microphone

Proximity—a nearness in space or time

Remote recording—recording done at a location other than a recording studio

Reverberation—prolongation of a sound; echo

Soundboard—a mixer or audio mixing board

Sound source—the group or item producing sound for recording

Stereo image—sound that is directed through two or more speakers so that it seems to surround the listener

Supercardioid—a microphone with a narrow heart-shaped polar pattern

Unidirectional—moving or operating in a single direction

X/Y—a coincident recording pattern designed to replicate a pair of human ears

Index